The Thessalonian Epistles

Genesis—Leon J. Wood
Exodus—F. B. Huey, Jr.
Leviticus—Louis Goldberg
Numbers—F. B. Huey, Jr.
Deuteronomy—Louis Goldberg
Joshua—Paul P. Enns
Judges—Paul P. Enns
Ruth—Paul P. Enns
1, 2 Samuel—Howard F. Vos
1 2 Kings—Howard F. Vos
1, 2 Chronicles—Eugene H. Merrill
Ezra, Nehemiah, Esther—Howard F. Vos
Job—D. David Garland
*Psalms— Ronald B. Allen
Proverbs—Eldon Woodcock
Ecclesiastes—Louis Goldberg
Song of Songs—Edward M. Curtis
Isaiah—D. David Garland
Jeremiah—F. B. Huey, Jr.
Lamentations—Dan G. Kent
Ezekiel—Paul P. Enns
Daniel—Leon J. Wood
Hosea—D. David Garland
Joel—Ronald B. Allen
Amos—D. David Garland
Obadiah, Jonah—John H. Walton and Bryan E. Beyer
Micah—Jack R. Riggs
Nahum, Habakkuk, Zephaniah, Haggai—J. N. Boo Heflin
Zechariah—Homer Heater, Jr.
Malachi—Charles D. Isbell
Matthew—Howard F. Vos
Mark—Howard F. Vos
Luke—Virtus E. Gideon
John—Herschel H. Hobbs
Acts—Curtis Vaughan
Romans—Curtis Vaughan and Bruce Corley
1 Corinthians—Curtis Vaughan and Thomas D. Lea
2 Corinthians—Aída B. Spencer and William D. Spencer
Galatians—Curtis Vaughan
Ephesians—Curtis Vaughan
Philippians—Howard F. Vos
Colossians and Philemon—Curtis Vaughan
The Thessalonian Epistles—John F. Walvoord
The Pastoral Epistles—E. M. Blaiklock
Hebrews—Leon Morris
James—Curtis Vaughan
1, 2 Peter, Jude—Curtis Vaughan and Thomas D. Lea
1, 2, 3 John—Curtis Vaughan
Revelation—Alan F. Johnson

*Not yet published as of this printing.

BIBLE STUDY COMMENTARY

The Thessalonian Epistles

JOHN F. WALVOORD

Lamplighter Books Grand Rapids, Michigan
Zondervan Publishing House

Lamplighter Books are published by Zondervan
Publishing House, 1415 Lake Drive, S.E.,
Grand Rapids, Michigan 49506

ISBN 0-310-34071-3

Printed in the United States of America

91 92 93 94 95 / EP / 26 25 24 23 22

Contents

Chapter   *Page*

Preface 7

I. Salvation in Relation to the Coming
of the Lord (1 Thess. 1:10) 11

II. Serving the Coming Lord
(1 Thess. 2:1-20) 19

III. Unblamable in Holiness
(1 Thess. 3:1—4:12) 28

IV. The Translation of the Church
(1 Thess. 4:13-18) 38

V. The Day of the Lord (1 Thess. 5:1-11) 49

VI. Christian Testimony in the Light of the
Lord's Return (1 Thess. 5:12-28) 57

VII. Glorifying God in Tribulation
(2 Thess. 1:1-12) 64

VIII. The Revelation of the Man of Sin
(2 Thess. 2:1-12) 72

IX. Chosen to Salvation (2 Thess. 2:13-17) 82

X. Serving and Waiting (2 Thess. 3:1-18) 89

Preface

The Thessalonian epistles as the first of the Pauline letters have a special place of their own in the New Testament. In many ways, they constitute an introduction to Christian doctrine. Each chapter is alive with vibrant truth especially pertinent to young believers. The great doctrines of salvation by grace, divine election, principles of effective Christian testimony, the coming of the Lord, divine judgment, and the joy and peace of fellowship with Christ are dominant themes. The epistles are at once doctrinal and practical, suited both to the demands of the mind and of the heart.

The exposition of First Thessalonians was published in *The Moody Monthly* in six installments, beginning in October 1954. Many requests received from readers encouraged the author to present the exposition of both epistles in this volume. Grateful acknowledgment is made of the kind permission of *The Moody Monthly* to reprint the material with some revision. The exposition of Second Thessalonians appears in print here for the first time.

An attempt has been made in this volume to bring out in a practical way the great truths contained in both letters. The presentation has the ordinary reader in mind. While technicalities have been avoided, advanced students of the Word will find, however, that the major problems of the epistles have been given adequate treatment. It is hoped that the publication of this volume will do something to correct the current neglect of the Thessalonian epistles, perhaps caused by the difficult problems arising in a popular exposition. It is the author's desire that this unfolding of divine revelation as contained in the Thessalonian epistles will prove a blessing to earnest students of the Word and will encourage further study of these messages to the young Thessalonian Christians.

The Thessalonian Epistles

CHAPTER 1

Salvation in Relation to the Coming of the Lord

FIRST THESSALONIANS 1:1-10

BACKGROUND OF THE EPISTLE

Thessalonica in the time of Paul was a thriving commercial town astride an important trade route. It had been founded in 316 B.C. by Cassander, King of Macedonia, who named it in honor of his wife, Thessalonica, the half sister of the famous Alexander the Great. Like Esther and Ruth in the Old Testament, the Thessalonian epistles trace their name to a famous woman.

When the Apostle Paul accompanied by Silas and Timothy entered Thessalonica, it was probably the first gospel witness ever given there. Acts seventeen records the amazing results of their ministry of less than a month. In those few short weeks, a small group of Thessalonians came to know Jesus Christ as Savior. Persecution that broke out almost immediately forced Paul and his companions to leave after ministering for three Sabbath days. Some months later, after he had heard of their continued faithfulness to Christ in the midst of persecution, Paul sent them this communication known to us as his First Epistle to the Thessalonians, in which he gives them encouragement and reminds them of his love and faithful prayer for them.

REMARKABLE FEATURES OF THE EPISTLE

There are a number of reasons why First Thessalonians is of special interest to believers in Christ today. One of the important reasons is that it is the first inspired letter written by Paul. As a letter addressed to young Christians, it is significant of the rich doctrinal content of Pauline teaching. Many important truths pertaining to the Christian life are unfolded in the letter, and in every chapter the theme of the coming of the Lord is prominent.

The first chapter unfolds the great theme of the Lord's coming in relation to *salvation*. In Chapter 2 the Lord's coming in relation to Christian *service* is presented. Chapter 3 relates *sanctification* to the Lord's coming. In Chapter 4 the Lord's coming is revealed as the *surety* of resurrection of our loved ones who have died in Christ. Chapter 5, which concludes the epistle, deals with the *safety* of the believer in the days of the wrath of God preceding the second coming of Christ. Throughout the epistle the theme of the coming of the Lord is related to practical Christian living.

The richness of the teaching of the Apostle Paul is evident as we study First Thessalonians. Though the Thessalonians were young Christians with less than a year of Christian experience, nevertheless they were familiar with the great and deep truths of the Christian faith, such as salvation, sanctification, assurance, the Trinity, the nature of man, resurrection, and the Day of the Lord. It is hard to realize as one reads First Thessalonians that the Christians to whom it was addressed had no New Testament. It is doubtful if they had any large portion of the Old Testament. They were immature Christians, with many trials and difficulties, and enduring much persecution. In the midst of their tribulations some of their number had gone on to be with the Lord, and with this in view Paul is writing them this letter of comfort, exhortation, and instruction.

OPENING SALUTATION

Chapter 1 opens with a very simple salutation: "Paul, and Silvanus, and Timotheus, unto the church of the Thessalonians." It is noteworthy that here, just as in 2 Thessalonians 2:1, there is an absence of all apostolic titles. There are only the simple names, Paul, and Silvanus — which was just another name for Silas — and Timotheus, which was another name for Timothy. The three of them had been the ones who had given the gospel to the Thessalonians. Timothy later had made one trip back to Thessalonica and had reported to Paul concerning what he had discovered (1 Thess. 3:1-6). The report was an epic of the steadfastness and faithfulness of the Thessalonian Christians. Paul was told that in spite of persecution the Thessalonians had a good testimony for Jesus Christ and were bearing high the gospel message.

GRACE AND PEACE

In the first verse of First Thessalonians there is quite a contrast between what the church at Thessalonica was as far as *state* is concerned — that is, persecution, uncertainty, and trouble — and the *position* that they had in Christ. Paul addresses them as the church of the Thessalonians which is "in God the Father and in the Lord Jesus Christ." Nothing could change their position — it included everything that was theirs because of being in Christ. It was true no matter what happened. But they needed more than this position.

Paul prays for them: "Grace be unto you, and peace." How rich are the simple words "grace" and "peace." Those without grace and peace are in utter poverty though they may possess all the riches of the world. Those with grace and peace are infinitely rich, though enduring persecution and sorrow, like the Thessalonians. Grace expressed the whole of God's love and favor in Christ. Peace with God and the peace of God is the priceless possession of the child of God. What richer jewels from God's treasures could be asked for anyone than "grace" and "peace"? While in a sense they already had grace and peace, they needed its manifestation, its experience, its triumph.

THANKS TO GOD ALWAYS

The Apostle begins with a burst of praise, more or less the theme of the whole epistle, his thankfulness to God for saving these Thessalonians through faith in Christ. He breathed out from his very heart in verse 2: "We give thanks to God always for you all, making mention of you in our prayers." Again something of the faithfulness of the prayer ministry of the Apostle Paul is indicated: "We give thanks to God always." In the days and the months which had passed since he left this little band of Thessalonians Paul had been faithful in prayer. What a rebuke it is to many of us who serve the Lord that often our hearts are not burdened with the needs of God's people nor thankful for the Lord's grace in their lives, especially when they are out of sight and out of mind. But Paul gives his testimony: "We give thanks to God always for you all."

This expression "for you all" is a very significant one. "You all" is used in the southern United States as an expansive, general expression referring to one person or many. Paul, however, uses it very accurately here. He was thanking God for *all* of them. In each life and heart the Spirit of God had wrought His work in such a way that souls had been saved and were now bearing a faithful testimony for the Lord Jesus Christ. He did not thank God for only some of them, but he thanked God for all of them. As we consider our own life and testimony, do our pastors and our Sunday school teachers — those with whom we work in Christian service — thank God for us *always?* Certainly there is a challenge to be like the Thessalonian Christians and so to live before God and our fellow Christians that they may thank God always for us.

REMEMBERING WITHOUT CEASING

As Paul thanked God he prayed, "making mention of you in our prayers." As he prayed for the Thessalonians he rehearsed some of the great realities that comprise the salvation of the believer. The remaining verses of Chapter 1 constitute a simple outline. First of all, in verse 3, Paul remembers what God has done through them and in them. Second, in verses 4-9, on the basis of what God has done, Paul knows certain things. Third, in verse 10 he expresses the hope of Christian salvation.

As he recalled his experiences with these Christians at Thessalonica, he states in verse 3: "Remembering without ceasing your work of faith, and labour of love, and patience of hope in our Lord Jesus Christ, in the sight of God and our Father." There are three famous words in this verse, "faith, hope, love." Paul is not thanking the Lord simply because in the Thessalonians there was faith and hope and love, which certainly ought to characterize every Christian. He is thanking God for what these three things had produced.

It is impossible to see faith, or love, or hope; they are immaterial things. But they can be manifested in a very definite physical way. It is this of which he speaks. "Remembering without ceasing your work of faith." Sometimes works and faith are contrasted, but here they are one and the same. A true faith is manifested in what we do. A true faith produces works. That is why James writes that faith without works is dead. It is not that works is a substitute for faith, but true faith in Christ will bring a real salvation which will in turn change the works of the believer in Christ. Not only was there a work of faith, but there was a labor of love. Love is more than a sentiment. It is a driving force in the heart of the believer who loves the Lord, and because he loves the Lord he is willing to labor; he is willing to work where it is difficult; he is willing to bear the burden.

Added to the labor of love was hope, and not simply hope, but hope that produced patience. What kind of hope is it that produces patience? The kind of hope that produces patience is a calm, sure, trusting hope. The reason that Christians can have patience in hope is because they are sure that our hope in Christ will be fulfilled. Thus it was in the Thessalonian church. They not only hoped in God but hope wrought patience in their hearts even in the time of trial and affliction which had overtaken them.

Verse 3 concludes with something that is most significant. It tells us that Paul regards their work of faith, and labor of love, and patience of hope in our Lord Jesus Christ not simply as he saw these things, but as they were in the sight of God and our Father. This brings us to a very pointed question which every one of us can ask ourselves: "What does God see in our hearts?" A real trust in Him? A real love for Him? A real hope for that which is a part of our Christian faith? Paul saw the outward evidence of these things, but God looks at the heart. Paul was able to commend these Christians in Thessalonica as he remembered not only what he saw, but what he knew that God saw in their hearts and lives.

KNOWING YOUR ELECTION

The second great theme of Paul's thankfulness to God was what he *knew* about them. There were some things that he knew about these Thessalonian believers because they had trusted in God and received His wonderful salvation. In verse 4 attention is called to this: "Knowing, brethren beloved of God, your election" (A.S.V.). How can a person know that somebody else is one of the elect of God? It was amazing that the Thessalonian Christians had been instructed in this doctrine of election, considering the short time that Paul and the others had ministered to them. Many Christians who have gone to church all their lives in our modern day know very little about the doctrine of election. The Bible indicates that God not only saves us, but that He chose us before the foundation of the world. It is a doctrine often not understood completely but believed because the Bible teaches it. Christians are the elect of God because God chose them before they chose Him. But how can anyone know the elect of God? Who of us have ever seen the Book of Life? How can one really know that his brethren are the elect of God?

BASIS OF ASSURANCE

The verses which follow give the basis of Paul's faith in connection with the Thessalonian Christians and, at the same time, give the basis for our faith and assurance that God is able to save those who trust in Christ. In verse 5 Paul writes: "Our gospel came not unto you in word only, but also in power, and in the Holy Ghost, and in much assurance." In other words, one of the reasons why he believed that they were really saved and why he knew their election was of God was the way the gospel came to them. It came in power and in the Holy Ghost and in much assurance — literally, "in full measure." It had not been simply an emotional experience nor had they been swept off their feet by Paul's oratory. This was unmistakably the power of the Holy Spirit at work. Further, it had been confirmed by the way Paul and his companions had lived among them. He reminds them of this when he goes on, "as ye know what manner of men we were among you for your sake." The power of God had been clearly manifested in their lives as well as in their testimony.

The crowning evidence was in the way the Word was received. It is one thing to preach the Word; it is another thing to receive the Word. In verse 6 there are three things noted concerning the way they received the Word. First, they received it in such a way that they became followers of Paul, "Ye became followers of us, and of the Lord." Second, they received the Word in much affliction. They did not receive the Word because it was easy to receive; they received it in spite of the persecution they knew would follow. Third, they received the Word with joy of the Holy Ghost. In other words, in spite of affliction, in spite of trial, there was the evidence of the ministry of the Holy Spirit in their hearts. They had the unspeakable joy of the Holy Spirit. The Word was received in such a way that they knew and Paul knew that they were really saved.

RESULTING LIFE OF TESTIMONY

Then, we have the capstone of it all. The Thessalonians not only had the Word come to them, they not only had received the Word of God, but their salvation was manifested in their life and testimony. In other words, as they had really trusted in Christ, it resulted in such a transformation of their lives that they became examples to all who believe. Verses 7 and 8 summarize it, "So that ye were ensamples [literally, *types* or *examples*] to all that believe in Macedonia and Achaia. For from you sounded out the word of the Lord not only in Macedonia and Achaia [that was the area in which they lived], but also in every place your faith to God-ward is spread abroad; so that we need not to speak any thing."

In other words, Paul was not required to tell people about how wonderfully God had been working in the Thessalonian church. The testimony went out everywhere without his help. One of the reasons for this was that Thessalonica was on a trade route, and people passing through Thessalonica came in contact with the aggressive evangelism and testimony of these Christians who lived in Thessalonica. In our day many folks come and go in our cities and towns and never come in contact with any vital Christianity. That apparently was not true in Thessalonica, for as the word spread it was widely known that God had done a wonderful work. The Thessalonians were preaching the Word, and everywhere the testimony of their faith to God was spread abroad.

TURNING TO GOD FROM IDOLS

Paul was told how God had worked in the Thessalonians. It had resulted in their turning to God from idols to serve the living and the true God. This is a very accurate expression and one that we should understand. It does not say that they turned from idols to God. Rather, they turned *to* God *from* idols to serve the living and true God. It was not reformation first and faith in Christ second, but it was faith in Christ first with the result that idols were forsaken. The tense of the word *turned,* as it is found in the Greek New Testament, is in the aorist which means that they turned once for all. It was a single, definite act. In a single, deliberate choice, they turned to God from idols. It was not simply that they were trusting God but the result of it was that they served the living and the true God. As Paul thinks on the faith and testimony of these Thessalonian Christians, young as they were, ignorant of many truths that we know today, there was, nevertheless, assurance in his heart that they were really saved. He knew that they were brethren beloved of God; he knew their election of God by the evidence of the transforming work of salvation manifested in their changed lives.

WAITING FOR HIS SON FROM HEAVEN

Not only did these believers have salvation in this wonderful manifestation, but they also had a glorious hope. One of the most precious things about the Christian hope is that it goes on and on and on. It is not something only for the present, but it is something for the future. In verse 10 the truth of the Lord's coming is introduced — a truth prominent in First Thessalonians in succeeding chapters.

It is significant that Paul in such a brief period of ministry not only led them out of darkness into the light in the gospel, but also faithfully preached to them the truth of the coming of the Lord. By contrast today, some folks who go to church year after year never hear the precious truth that Christ who came to Bethlehem so long ago is coming again and that we can be looking for that wonderful return of the Lord for His own. So in verse 10 he reminds the believers in Thessalonica that they not only have turned to God from idols to serve the living and true God — a present work — but they also have a new hope for the future: "And to wait for His Son from heaven." The word "wait" is in the present tense. They had turned to God in one act, but there remained the constant, day by day expectation. In other words, they were constantly looking for the return of the Lord, the coming of the Lord for His saints.

DELIVERED FROM WRATH

The chapter closes with the reminder that the Lord Jesus Christ, the one who is coming, the one "whom he raised from the dead, even Jesus," the Savior, "delivered us from the wrath to come." In one short verse there are gathered the great doctrines of the second coming of Christ, "waiting for His Son from heaven"; the resurrection of Christ, "whom he raised from the dead"; and the salvation that Christ wrought in His first coming when He died on the cross, "which delivered us from the wrath to come."

Wrath is coming! The closing chapter of First Thessalonians brings this very graphically before us. There is a day of judgment coming. There is a time when God is going to judge this sinful world. Christ on Calvary nineteen hundred years ago delivered us from the wrath to come, that is, He delivered all who would trust in Him, all who would receive the Lord Jesus Christ as personal Savior. These Thessalonians who lived so long ago had come into the glorious truth that Christ had died for them. They were delivered from the wrath to come. For them the coming of the Lord was a glorious event to which they could look with keen anticipation and with hearts that were filled with expectation.

THE CHALLENGE

This first chapter of First Thessalonians constitutes a real challenge to every thinking Christian. It is first of all a challenge for us to ask, "What do people think of us when they pray for us?" Do they remember our work of faith, our labor of love, and our patience of hope? When they think of us, are they assured of our salvation? Do they see in our lives the evidence that the Word of God has come in power, that we have been transformed, that we have been made followers of the Lord Jesus Christ, that we exercise our faith in the midst of affliction, that we have the evidence of the joy of the Holy Spirit and a transformed life so that our testimony is spread abroad? Is that true of us? And is it true of us, like the Thessalonians, that there is the living hope of the coming of the Lord, the same one who loved us, who died for our sins that He might deliver us from the wrath to come, and who was raised in victory over the grave? Yes, this letter was written many years ago, to Christians who long since have left the earthly scene, but the truth lives on. May the truth of this chapter not only live in the written pages of the Word of God, but may it be manifested in our hearts and in our daily lives.

Questions

1. What do we know about the background of Thessalonica and the situation there when Paul arrived?
2. Why is 1 Thessalonians of special interest?
3. What five words characterize the five chapters of 1 Thessalonians?
4. How would you contrast the state and position of the Thessalonians?
5. How is Paul an example to us in thanksgiving and prayer?
6. What was the basis of Paul's assurance of their salvation?
7. What did Paul reveal to them concerning the nature of their hope?

CHAPTER 2

Serving the Coming Lord

FIRST THESSALONIANS 2:1-20

SALVATION FIRST

Over the first chapter the word "salvation" was written because this letter would never have been written if the Thessalonians had not trusted in the Lord Jesus. It was the beginning of vital living for God, of entering into eternal things. It is a reminder, of course, that one does not begin living until he is saved by trusting the Lord Jesus Christ. Life begins when that greatest of all decisions is made of trusting in Jesus Christ as personal Savior.

There are many today who have religion, that is, they go to church and engage in religious activities. But it is only too true that many have only the outer appearance of Christianity and have never come to real faith in Jesus Christ as personal Savior. The Thessalonians were not guilty of superficial religion, however. They had really trusted Christ and their lives had been transformed. The fact of their salvation lays the foundation for the truths which are revealed in the chapters which follow.

A SUCCESS STORY

Over Chapter 2 can be written a very common word, "service." The chapter reveals how to serve God both by precept and by Paul's dynamic example. Chapter 2 of First Thessalonians is a "success story." Paul had done something that was quite phenomenal. He had come to a town where there was not a single Christian. He had gone into the Jewish synagogue and there had preached the gospel. He had preached also to Gentiles in their homes. In three weeks this dynamic person by the grace of God had founded a new church — a church which has come down through the centuries to us as an example of faith and faithfulness. How did he do it?

There are many communities in America that need desperately churches bearing a real testimony for Christ. Can we have such churches? The answer is found in the second chapter of First Thessalonians. Paul begins chapter 2 with the fact of their testimony being used of God: "For yourselves, brethren, know our entrance in unto you, that it was not in vain." God had undertaken for them and blessed the message and souls were saved. In verse 2 the secret of it is revealed.

19

BOLDNESS IN TESTIMONY

Over the first two verses of the second chapter we can write the word *boldness*. One of the reasons why Paul was successful was that he was bold. If he had gone to Thessalonica and had failed to preach the gospel, the probability is that in three weeks he would not have made much of an impression. If he had not told anyone about the Lord Jesus Christ, if he had not proclaimed boldly that Christ was the only Savior, that Christ loved the world, that He died for the world, that they could be saved only by trusting in the risen Savior, he would not have had one convert.

BOLDNESS IN SPITE OF SUFFERING

The first point in effective service for God is boldness, a boldness made more significant by subjection to suffering. Paul and Silas had come from Philippi where they had been thrown into prison, and beaten, and had suffered for the gospel's sake. When Paul came to Thessalonica, instead of saying "I have suffered enough" — as some Christians might have done — he spoke boldly. Hence in verse 2 we read, "Even after that we had suffered before, and were shamefully entreated, as ye know, at Philippi, we were bold in our God to speak unto you the gospel of God with much contention."

The word that is translated "bold" comes from a Greek word of eight syllables, *eparresiasametha*. It is a long word. It means to be bold in the sense of speaking out publicly, of making a public declaration. It is possible to be a secret believer. Undoubtedly, some are saved that have not told very many about it. But secret believers do not lead souls to Christ. The way to lead people to Christ is to be *bold*, to proclaim the gospel. This is the basic program of the present dispensation.

BOLDNESS WITH AGONY OF HEART

Paul was called to preach and he preached boldly, "with much contention." The word which is translated "contention" is *agoni*. It is the word from which we get *agony*. There was an agony of soul in Paul as he preached the gospel. To be effective in our testimony, to be successful even by worldly standards, it is necessary to have a boldness inspired by an agony of heart. This does not mean that one should be tactless, or without common sense in the approach, but there must be a bold witness for Jesus Christ.

PREACHING THE PURE WORD

In 1 Thessalonians 2:3-6, the character of Paul's preaching is graphically portrayed. One of the tragedies of our day, as all true Bible students know, is that some preaching is not according to the Word of God. Like the ancient Bereans, modern Christians need to search the Scriptures, testing the message by the Book. By this standard, Paul's preaching rang true. This was evident first by the things that were not true about his preaching. In verse 3

Paul writes, "Our exhortation was not of deceit, nor of uncleanness, nor in guile." In other words, it was pure in its *content* and in its *intent*. It was pure in the sense that there was no deceit or, literally, no error. There was no uncleanness or impurity of motive either.

DANGER OF ADULTERATING THE WORD

Sometimes truth is mixed with error. In fact, the most dangerous kind of preaching is that which is partly true. But Paul said, "my message was not just partly true. It is without error. It has no deceit in it. It is the pure truth. It is not adulterated by human philosophy and human speculation." It was, then, God's message to them concerning Christ.

Paul goes on to a further claim: his message was also without guile — that is, Paul did not come to trick them and to use methods that were question-able. He did not try to get a superficial decision for Christ, but he laid down plainly before them the truth of the gospel and the issues of heaven and hell that were concerned. The result was that when they trusted in Christ it was a clear-cut decision which resulted in a real testimony that stood the test in the days that followed. It depended upon the purity of the message in both its content and intent.

PLEASING GOD

It is also brought out that Paul was a faithful servant of God as he preached. "But as we were allowed of God to be put in trust with the gospel, even so we speak; not as pleasing men, but God, which trieth our hearts." The final test of every life and of every message or sermon is "What does God think about it?" The judgment of God is not always according to the judgment of men. Men may judge a message by its interest, its literary quality, the words delivered, its intelligence, the fact that the speaker revealed great background of knowledge in his subject, or by the skill with which it was delivered. When a preacher delivers a message for God it should be just as good as he can make it. On the other hand, God is primarily concerned with the message itself. Is it true? The most beautifully deli-vered sermon that is not true, that is not God's message, is useless in the hands of God.

The ultimate test of a message is, does it please God? That is true for the preacher, for the Sunday school teacher, or the personal worker. There is no more acid test of any service that is rendered for God than the question, "Is it pleasing to God?" Our little houses of self-praise and self-gratification tumble in a moment when we stop to consider "What does God think about it?" As Paul preached he said, "I was not trying to please you Thessalo-nians; I did not come here to impress upon you that I was a great pulpit orator, or a great missionary, or a great scholar. I was here because I was seeking to please God." Certainly this is a standard to challenge every thoughtful Christian.

TWIN EVILS OF FLATTERY AND COVETOUSNESS

Paul reveals how this worked out in verse 5: "Neither at any time used we flattering words, as ye know, nor a cloke of covetousness; God is witness." In this verse is seen, as was mentioned earlier, in Chapter 1, that Paul appeals sometimes to the outward, i.e., what *man* can see; sometimes he appeals to what *God* can see. It is not difficult for us to identify flattery. We all know people who are flatterers, and sometimes we like to listen to them. Some people delight to be told, "My, you look so young," and to hear the comment that they look fifteen years younger than they actually are. The flesh loves flattery. But Paul said, "I did not come to you Thessalonians and say, What outstanding citizens you are! What beautiful characters you are! Folks as good as you are ought to be trusting Christ." No, he did not use any flattery. He told them the hard truth, that they were lost sinners, that they were bound for hell, that they needed a Savior desperately, that their religion such as they had was not enough. They needed Christ; they needed His glorious salvation. There was no flattery in that, was there? That was the truth. He said, "I did not come to flatter you; I came to deliver a message from God." He reminds them of the fact that they knew it. There was no one in Thessalonica who thought of Paul as a flatterer.

But when it came to covetousness, there was something that pertains to the heart. It is not always apparent whether a person is covetous or not. It is difficult to determine whether one is serving you to make money or whether he is honestly trying to help you without covetousness. Paul does something here which is certainly the application of the acid test. He calls God to witness. "As God is my witness, I did not come here to make merchandise of you; I did not come because you promised me an honorarium, or a high salary, or any of the things that pertain to the comforts of life. I did not come that way to you and you know it. God is witness that my heart was right in this thing." Not only was his message pure in its content, but his whole purpose was pure in the sight of God. That, of course, was one of the reasons God could use him.

RENUNCIATION OF THE HONOR OF MEN

Verse 6 adds another important factor: "Nor of men sought we glory, neither of you, nor yet of others, when we might have been burdensome, as the apostles of Christ." In other words, Paul could have come to the Thessalonians and expanded his chest and said, "I am an apostle and you must recognize my high office because God has sent me." He could have told them he had the right to order them around, but he said, "I did not come in that spirit. I did not come to be honored by you. I came because I had a message, because I wanted to help you, because you needed the Savior."

Certainly that is the secret of effective Christian testimony. Boldness, having our hearts right before God, delivering God's message in its purity and in its power, seeking not our own advantage but seeking the glory and the approbation of God — that is the secret of Paul's success.

LOVING THE PEOPLE OF GOD

Through verse 6 Paul has itemized the things that he did *not* do. He was not covetous or deceitful and he did not have errors in his message. In verse 7 and through verse 12 we have what he did do — the positive side of his message. There is a danger of regarding Christianity as a negative standard. We should not do this; we should not do that; we should not do something else. There are bona fide negatives in the Christian faith. If one is going to have a real testimony for Christ, there are some things he cannot do. But Christianity does not consist in negatives. Christianity consists in what one believes, in the life one lives and in the service one renders. Paul is revealing here the secret why he was so effective in this Thessalonian church.

In verses 7-8 Paul shows his loving care for them: "But we were gentle among you, even as a nurse cherisheth her children: so being affectionately desirous of you, we were willing to have imparted unto you, not the gospel of God only, but also our own souls, because ye were dear unto us." Here is the compassionate heart that made possible the successful ministry of Paul.

In our service for God have we lost our heart? Sometimes we do things for God because it is our duty. If we cannot do it for any other reason, let us do it as our duty. But certainly there is something deeper than that. Paul had come to this city of Thessalonica, to those he had never seen before. But how he loved them now as trophies of grace! As a parent loves his child he loved these little ones of Christ.

Paul was taking care of them just as a nurse takes care of her children. Literally, the expression is a "nurse taking care of her own children." A professional nurse will often do a good job of taking care of someone else's child because she believes in a certain professional standard of duty. But if it is her own child, that makes a tremendous difference. All the technicalities now become tremendously important and she is willing, if necessary, to give her own life, as Paul says he is willing to do for the Thessalonians. Paul is revealing the compassion, the burning heart that he has as he deals with these whom he had led to know Jesus Christ as Savior.

LABORING NIGHT AND DAY

Paul reminds the Thessalonians also in verse 9 how he had labored in their midst: "Ye remember, brethren, our labour and travail: for labouring night and day, because we would not be chargeable unto any of you, we preached unto you the gospel of God." Paul did not have a forty-hour week. When it came to 4:30 or 5:00 o'clock, he did not say, "Now the rest of the day is mine; I can do with it as I please." No, Paul was a bondslave of Jesus Christ. He was under orders like a soldier whether it was eight hours or twelve hours or twenty-four hours. Paul was on duty, and as he realized that his time was short he "laboured night and day."

In apostolic times it was customary to stop work when darkness came and go to bed. When a person labored night and day it was the unusual thing, but that was what Paul did. Many a lonely hour in the night he was trying to help some soul come to Christ, to understand the tremendous issues that were latent in the gospel message, and praying with them. He was laboring night and day. There was many a late hour when Paul was alone on his knees before God getting the power and strength and the wisdom to know what to do the next day as he sought to be a true servant of God. The Christian life is not a continuous vacation. Christians should have vacations even as Christ took His disciples off to rest awhile. But the Christian life should not be a question of doing as little as possible. Rather like Paul our lives should be poured out in service for the Lord.

In verses 10-11 he reminds them of his faithful labors: "Ye are witnesses, and God also, how holily and justly and unblameably we behaved ourselves among you that believe: as ye know how we exhorted and comforted and charged every one of you, as a father doth his children." Earlier Paul used the figure of a nurse caring for her child, a mother's love if you please; now he turns to a different figure, a father's love for his children. Both were true in the Apostle's heart. His labor and his ministry were honorable before God who sees the heart. Seeking to win others for Christ is not only a matter of boldness in the spoken message. There must also be the attendant life of testimony for God. Few Christians realize how many are watching them to discover in their lives the answer to the question of whether Christianity is real, whether it really satisfies, and whether it pays to serve the Lord. Paul, as he ministered to the Thessalonians, not only delivered the message in word but he delivered the message also in life. His daily life before them was the life of a man who was walking in the will of God.

WALKING WORTHY

Paul concludes this section, therefore, in verse 12, with the exhortation "That ye would walk worthy of God, who hath called you unto his kingdom and glory." Christians are in the kingdom of God now, but there is a glorious kingdom ahead of us also, the glory that is going to be ours in the predicted millennial kingdom and throughout eternity as we are with Christ. In view of these things, God has called us to a walk that is in keeping with our destiny. A little child born into a royal family is given special care. He cannot do the things that other children do, at least not in quite the same way. The reason is that he is being prepared for a place of responsibility and leadership.

Christians are exactly in that position. We do not "walk worthy" in order to be saved, or in order to become a royal child, but we "walk worthy" of God because we are saved, because we are a child of the King by grace through faith in the Lord Jesus Christ. So Paul lays before the Thessalonian Christians this exhortation to "walk worthy." How many problems this standard solves! Sometimes folks will come to a preacher or a Sunday school teacher and say: "Now, is this right? Can a Christian do this?" So many of those problems are solved in a moment if the question is asked: "Is it worthy? Is it something that is honoring to God? Would God be pleased with this situation? So often the uncertainties and the obscurities in the judgment of men are wiped away when one applies the test of the Scriptures. Certainly there are many things that we cannot do as Christians because we are Christians, because God has called us to a holy walk and a life that is well pleasing to Him.

RECEIVING THE WORD AS FROM GOD

In the closing portion of Chapter 2, beginning with verse 13, the other side of the picture is presented. In the first eleven verses Paul's secret of success is unfolded — why he preached, how he preached, and why he had such phenomenal results. There are two aspects to every sermon; one is the delivery and the other is the hearing. How do we listen to sermons? We listen to sermons from different standpoints. A preacher may listen to a sermon to see if he can get a message for some future occasion. A Sunday school teacher may listen to a sermon to see if he can get some information for his Sunday school lesson. A person who is lonely may be coming for comfort. A person who is unsaved may be seeking salvation. There are different motives behind our hearing. Sometimes our motives are not good. Sometimes Christians do not really come with open hearts to receive a message from God, and become occupied with the messenger instead of the message and the Savior.

The Thessalonian Christians, according to the record, were not simply interested in Paul, as grand a figure as he was, but as he delivered the message recorded in these verses they received it as the Word of God. Verse 13 notes: "For this cause also thank we God without ceasing, because, when ye received the word of God which ye heard of us, ye received it not as the word of men, but as it is in truth, the word of God, which effectually worketh also in you that believe." The message was received not because Paul delivered it. The thing that thrilled them was that they had heard the Word of God. They had received it as the authoritative Word of God because it came from God. The proof of it is found in the verses that follow.

PERSECUTION A TEST OF FAITH

Testing had come almost at once for this new band of Christians and they were bitterly persecuted. Paul tells them that they became followers of others who were persecuted. "Ye, brethren, became followers of the churches of God which in Judaea are in Christ Jesus: for ye also have suffered like things of your own countrymen, even as they have of the Jews." One of the hardest experiences in life when you stand for Christ is to have your own loved ones oppose you. If friends and neighbors and relatives — one's own loved ones — oppose a young Christian, it makes it very difficult, but this was often true in the early church. It is also true in modern times. What a young Christian does under these circumstances is a test of the reality of his faith. The Thessalonians had stood true, no matter who opposed them.

Persecution was not peculiar to the Thessalonians however. Paul mentions the fact that those who lived in Jerusalem at that time had "killed the Lord Jesus, and their own prophets, and have persecuted us; and they please not God, and are contrary to all men." You see Paul, who was a Jew, was being persecuted by his fellow countrymen just as Christ had been crucified before by His own people. The Thessalonians were going through a similar experience. Opposition to the apostles had gone so far as to be described in verse 16 as "forbidding us to speak to the Gentiles that they might be saved, to fill up their sins alway: for the wrath is come upon them to the uttermost." The opposition of the world and of the unbelieving heart is especially brought out when a person faithfully preaches Christ. The world does not necessarily oppose morality as such. It often does not oppose religion as such, but it does oppose a bona fide, transforming kind of Christianity. The world does not want Christ and Him crucified. When we take our stand for Christ, we can expect some opposition from unbelievers.

PAUL'S LONGING FOR THEM

Paul opens his heart in verses 17 and 18 as he tells them how he longed after them. When we have loved ones who are away from us and we get word that they are going through the deep waters of affliction, how we want to drop everything and rush to them! We think they need us, and our comfort and help. Paul was just that way, but he could not go back. If he had gone back, he would have become a martyr for the faith. He would have cut short a ministry that God had for him. It was not God's will for Paul to die at this point in his life. For this reason, he could not go to Thessalonica. Satan hindered him. How Satan sometimes gets in our way! This word *hinder* in the Greek means *to break up the road*. The thought is that the way was impassable. Satan had broken up the road before him and Paul could not get through to them, even though he longed to see them and to be a further help to them.

WHAT IS OUR HOPE?

But all was not lost. In verses 19 and 20 there is a bright note, repeated so often in this epistle, the theme of the coming of the Lord and the joy that will be ours when Christ comes back. Paul asks in verse 19, "What is our hope?" What does the future hold for us? Do we have a real hope? A person who is a Christian has a real hope. One who has been born again, who is a child of God, has a real hope. But if our hope is not in Christ we have no ground for hope. Paul said, "What is our hope, or joy, or crown of rejoicing?"

WHAT IS OUR CROWN OF REJOICING?

Paul is looking forward to that glad day when this life's journey will be over and he would be in the presence of the Lord along with all the other Christians. He is picturing the time of the translation of the church, when Christ will come for His own to take them home to glory. He had asked, What is our hope, our joy, our crown of rejoicing? The answer is: "Are not even ye in the presence of our Lord Jesus Christ at his coming? For ye are our glory and joy." Paul was not content to be saved himself. It is wonderful to be saved; it is wonderful to know one is going to heaven. But Paul said the real joy that was going to be in his heart as he stood in the presence of the Lamb of God, the one who loved him, the one who had died for him on the cross, would be his spiritual children that he would bring with him, whom he had led to know Jesus Christ as Savior.

Have you ever led a soul to Christ? One may say, "I am not an evangelist. I am not a good personal worker." But have you ever tried? God loves to use those who are willing to be used, and there is latent in many a Christian a gift for leading souls to Christ which he does not realize. Almost anyone can give out gospel tracts. Any Christian can pray. Anyone can give of his substance for missions. There are more ways than one by which earnest Christians can lead souls to Christ. When that glad day comes when we are in the presence of Christ, will we have some trophies of grace? Paul said, "When that day comes, I am going to be exalted. Why? Because of you Thessalonians who came to know the Lord Jesus Christ through my ministry among you." In that day, will it be our portion to look at those saved through our gospel testimony and with Paul to say, "Ye are our glory and joy"?

Questions

1. Why is this chapter a success story?
2. What do we learn about boldness?
3. Explain how Paul's message was pure in content and intent.
4. Contrast Paul's desire to please God and his approach to pleasing men.
5. Contrast what Paul did not do with what he did do in presenting his message to them.
6. How does Paul describe the response of the Thessalonians to his message?
7. How does Chapter 2 end on a message of hope?

CHAPTER 3

Unblamable in Holiness
FIRST THESSALONIANS 3:1 — 4:12

BACKGROUND OF CHAPTER THREE

In the first chapter of 1 Thessalonians, the great theme of *salvation* was unfolded. There is nothing in all the world that thrills the heart like a real experience of trust in the Lord Jesus, which the Thessalonians had experienced. Chapter 2 presented the challenge of Christian *service*. Paul speaks of his own service and the rules of ministry, as well as the service and faithfulness of the Thessalonian church as it will be recognized at the judgment seat of Christ in glory. Chapter 3, before us now, has the theme of *sanctification,* which continues into Chapter 4 through verse 12.

THE GOOD TIDINGS FROM THESSALONICA

In 1 Thessalonians 3:1-10 Paul relates the testimony of the Thessalonian church as it was brought to him. In a word, this is what happened: When Paul was meditating upon the need of the Thessalonian church and his heart was burdened in prayer for them, he had sent Timothy back to find out how they were getting along. He is described as "our brother, and minister of God, and our fellow-labourer in the gospel of Christ." Gracious words here from the great apostle! The purpose of sending Timothy was "to establish you, and to comfort you concerning your faith." Timothy was to do what Paul longed to do himself, but could not. Paul wanted the Thessalonians to continue steadfast in spite of affliction of which Paul states, "We are appointed thereunto." He was concerned lest the trial uncover superficiality in their faith and "our labour be in vain."

Timothy had gone to Thessalonica and had brought encouragement to them, continuing to teach them the Word of God. Now Timothy has returned to Paul with the message that the Thessalonians were standing fast in the faith, that they longed to see Paul, that they were just as he had left them — their hearts fixed upon the Lord Jesus Christ and looking for His coming. Paul's own heart overflowed as he contemplated the goodness of God in blessing his testimony there and working so abundantly in the lives of these Thessalonians.

PAUL'S GREAT HEART

There are a number of things that could be said about this portion of Scripture. Paul recites how he was comforted and how the tidings came. It is summed up more or less in verse 8: "For now we live, if ye stand fast in the Lord." More expressively translated, it states: "Now we are really living, if you are standing fast in the faith." In other words, his whole spiritual joy and happiness is linked with the experience of victory in this Thessalonian church. Consider for a moment the background of this statement. How interested and how concerned would we be if we had been in Paul's position? Paul had been there just a few weeks and had led these few souls to Christ, but now it seems that his very life depended upon the success and the prosperity of this church. His whole heart was wrapped up in the spiritual prosperity of these his children in the faith.

What a challenge this should be to us that we may have that same sensitivity of the soul, that we may have that passion, that love which was in the heart of Christ Himself for the sheep, for the people of God. In the Bible, men of God, men who really served God had a heart for the needs of souls. Too often in our modern life our theology is in one compartment and our heart is in another. We believe that souls are lost without Christ and recognize human suffering and human need, but it is never translated into prayer, or into helpfulness, or into doing what we can to meet the needs of others. What a contrast to Paul!

In verses 9 and 10 we get a picture of Paul's great heart. "For what thanks can we render to God again for you, for all the joy wherewith we joy for your sakes before our God; night and day praying exceedingly that we might see your face, and might perfect that which is lacking in your faith?" Here is the compassionate heart of Paul toward the Thessalonian believers and his concern lest they lack something of completion of their spiritual faith and experience. Modern Christians are so prone to ignore a need like this. While recognizing that so many Christians are ignorant of the great truths of Scripture and are not going on with the Lord, they do not have a real prayer life; they do not give themselves to the study of the Word; they are not soul winners. It is a tragedy that in our hearts there can be such coldness and such a lack of response to spiritual need. What a challenge Paul is! In his own spiritual experience his heart is overflowing in praise to God for hearing his prayer. It was not just a few minutes or a few sentences of prayer, but he tells us here he spent hours, day and night, praying to God for the continuance and faithfulness of this little band of Christians. If we had prayer like that and if our hearts were stirred like Paul's, we would have a spiritual revival such as this nation has never seen. What we need is revival first of all in the hearts of the people of God.

The Challenge to Our Hearts

What does Paul say to us in this passage? He is saying that if we are really committed to the Lord — if we are really letting the Holy Spirit rule supremely in our hearts and lives — that there should be the evidence of the love of the Spirit and the compassion of the Spirit toward our fellow Christians as well as toward those who do not know the Lord Jesus. The challenge of this passage is to let the Spirit of God transform our hearts and make them tender, that we may not follow the pattern of this careless and indifferent generation which is unmindful of the spiritual needs of those about us.

Are we really concerned about souls? Do we pray for the salvation of that neighbor in the next apartment or in the next house? Are we concerned in our churches about the backsliders and the indifferent who are not serving the Lord as they should? Paul tells us that the secret is to pray. If we have a real burden of prayer we will have Paul's experience of the joy of answered prayer. Certainly these are important and most practical verses.

Increasing and Abounding in Love

In verses 11 and 12 Paul breathes another prayer that he might go back and see the Thessalonians again. "Now God himself and our Father, and our Lord Jesus Christ, direct our way unto you. And the Lord make you to increase and abound in love one toward another, and toward all men, even as we do toward you." In other words, Paul said: "Let us go on in our Christian faith." The most dangerous thing in our spiritual experience is to ease off and to rest on our oars. Normal Christian growth brings with it an increase in love to each other and to all men. While the Thessalonians were a model church, there was still room for growth and improvement.

Perfecting That Which Is Lacking

The coming of the Lord is mentioned again in verse 13. In Thessalonians every chapter deals with the Lord's coming. The last verse of Chapter 1 dealt with waiting for the Lord's return. Chapter 2 spoke of the presence of our Lord Jesus Christ at His coming in verse 19. The last verse of Chapter 3 deals once again with the coming of the Lord. Paul, as he is praying for these Thessalonian Christians, has in mind not only their present holiness, but also that they should go on to perfection.

In verse 10 the word *perfect* is mentioned, "That we . . . might perfect that which is lacking in your faith." There are some in our day who think that it is not possible to be saved unless one reaches a stage of moral perfection. They attribute to the word *perfect* ideas which are contrary to the Word of God. Paul was praying that "God might perfect that which is lacking." What did he mean? It seems clear that he was not doubting their salvation because he speaks of "knowing, brethren, your election" (1:4).

What Is Biblical Perfection?

There are two main ideas about perfection in the Bible. There is first of all the idea of perfection which is the thought of coming to the end of a journey or the fulfillment of a purpose or a design. It is fulfillment or perfection in the sense, for instance, of a perfect man, one who has grown through boyhood and youth until he has the full stature of a man. He is a perfect man in the sense that he has reached the goal of growth. He is perfect in the sense that he has completed the man. There is another word used for perfection which has the thought of *equipment*. It means *to be completely equipped,* in other words, the details are in order. A home, for instance, can be spoken of as being fully equipped. It has everything that a home ought to have: furniture, curtains, rugs, and everything else. It is perfectly equipped. This is what Paul had in mind here.

Perfection Never Means Sinless

Paul accordingly prayed that God might perfect that which was lacking in these Thessalonian Christians. Their faith needed to be enlarged. Their lives were not complete in their spiritual experience. Paul wanted God to deal with them and to bring them on to that further step of perfection. Nowhere in the Bible is the word *perfect* used to mean sinlessly perfect. In fact, that is not the idea at all. There is need for another word in English into which we could translate these words, because the word *perfection* in the ordinary sense is not exactly the idea. It is only the thought of completion or attainment but not the idea of sinless perfection. Paul is praying that the Thessalonians might be complete and in the end might stand unblamable in holiness before God.

Unblamable in Holiness

In verse 13 Paul's prayer for them is that they may abound in love "to the end he may stablish your hearts unblameable in holiness before God, even our Father, at the coming of our Lord Jesus Christ with all his saints." Some may recall how H. A. Ironside, that great expositor of Scripture, in his early years struggled with the problem of holiness, seeking earnestly an experience of complete sanctification. The story is told in his book, *Holiness, the False and the True,* in which he says he thought he had to be completely holy in order to be saved. Accordingly, he would have some experience and would believe he was saved and completely sanctified. He would go on for a week or two and then suddenly be aware that he was not perfect after all. Then he came to the conclusion that he was not saved. So he would do the whole thing over again. In this difficulty, he discovered Hebrews 12:14

where he read: "Follow peace with all men, and holiness, without which no man shall see the Lord." He reasoned correctly that when one follows he has not attained, but that it will be attained when we see the Lord.

This same thought is in 1 Thessalonians 3:13: "to the end that he may stablish your hearts unblameable in holiness before God, even our Father, at the coming of our Lord Jesus Christ with all his saints." While we are imperfect in this life, constantly falling short and having to come to God in confession of our sins, the day is coming when we shall be perfect, absolutely unblamable, not only in our position before God but in our spiritual state. That day will be when we stand before Christ at His coming. We are rightly concerned about our imperfections, but, thank God, if He has saved our soul He will never let us go until He has brought us to perfection which will be realized when Christ comes for His own. This is the great expectation behind Paul's prayer that these Thessalonians may grow in grace and attain the ultimate goal of being unblamable in holiness before Christ at His coming.

COMING EVENTS IN THE PROPHETIC WORD

Verse 13 has attracted students of the Word from another standpoint in regard to the expression, "at the coming of our Lord Jesus Christ with all his saints." Many Bible teachers teach, as does the writer, that the Lord is coming for His church at any time. We believe in the imminent return of Christ, that 1 Thessalonians 4 is going to be fulfilled, that the dead in Christ are going to arise, and that living Christians will be translated without dying into the presence of God. We further believe that after this event there will take place a great time of trouble in the world, predicted by Daniel and Christ Himself, culminating in the great tribulation. We believe that at the end of the great tribulation Christ is coming back in power and glory from heaven with the saints and with the holy angels and that He will establish His righteous government on the earth as predicted many times in the Bible, which will last, according to Revelation 20, for one thousand years and ultimately will be followed by the eternal state after the judgment of the great white throne.

Where does this passage fit into this background? Many expositors, in considering this particular expression, "at the coming [lit., *in* the coming] of our Lord Jesus Christ with all his saints," have distinguished His coming *for* His saints (the rapture) and His coming *with* His saints (the second coming to establish the millennial kingdom). While this is a bona fide distinction, it raises the question: "Just when will Christians be presented unblamable in holiness before God?" If we believe that Christ is coming before the great tribulation, we are going to be presented unblamable in holiness before God long before His second coming to set up His kingdom. If that is true, how can we explain this portion of Scripture?

THREE WORDS FOR THE COMING OF THE LORD

The secret of it is in the word *coming*. There are at least three great words in the New Testament used to express the truth about the coming of the Lord: *epiphaneia, apokalupsis,* and *parousia.* All three of these words are used of Christ coming for His church. They are also used of His coming to set up His kingdom on the earth. They are not technical words, then, but general words, and all of them have to do with the coming of Christ. One of them (*epiphaneia*) simply speaks of His appearing, that is, that we are going to see Him. We are told also that when Christ comes to set up His kingdom on the earth *every* eye will see Him.

There is another word (*apokalupsis*) translated *revelation.* It is the word used for the name of the last book of the New Testament, the Revelation of Jesus Christ in the sense of the revelation of His glory. When Christ came the first time He came in humiliation. His glory was veiled except on the Mount of Transfiguration and perhaps in the Garden of Gethsemane. In the latter place, when those who came to take Him asked if He was Jesus and He said "I am," they all fell before Him to the ground, apparently struck down by a momentary flash of the glory and authority of Christ. For the most part, however, His glory was veiled even after His resurrection. When He comes the second time we will see Him in His glory and this will be a *revelation.*

The word that is found here in 1 Thessalonians 3:13 is the third word, the Greek word *parousia,* which means *presence,* but is usually translated *coming.* This word is derived from two words: a preposition (*para*) meaning *along,* and *ousia* which is a form of the verb *to be;* hence the word means, *to be along side of,* or *to be present.* While commonly translated in the Bible by the word *coming,* the word itself does not strictly mean coming and is used with other meanings. It means *presence* and is so translated in 2 Corinthians 10:10 and Philippians 2:12.

What does this word *coming* or *presence* mean here in Thessalonians? When someone is coming, we also speak of his presence. For instance, a visiting preacher might be welcomed with the words, "We are happy for the coming of the Reverend John Doe." What would be meant by that? How he came would not be important; the point would be that he is here. What is meant is that we are glad for his presence. His coming was just the means to the end. Even in English we use the term *coming* in the sense of *presence.* That is precisely the thought here. But when are we going to be in the presence of the Father?

IN THE PRESENCE OF THE LORD

According to Scripture, Christians are going to meet Christ in the air. We are going to be present with Him at that moment. After we meet Him in the air, He will take us home to glory to be in the presence of the Father and the holy angels. After that we are coming back to the earth with Christ. This word *coming* here may not refer specifically to the coming of Christ with His saints to the earth, but rather the coming to heaven when they will be in the presence of the Father. That is the same thought considered in 2:19, "in the presence of our Lord Jesus Christ at his coming," literally, "before our Lord Jesus Christ in his presence." In 3:13, the verse, translated literally, reads, "before God, even our Father *in the presence* [italics supplied] of our Lord Jesus Christ with all his saints." There is a coming to the earth, but there is also the coming to heaven. What an event that arrival in heaven is going to be! All the holy angels will be in attendance on that day. When the dead in Christ and living Christians are caught up to be with the Lord and arrive in heaven as the trophies of grace, the marvels of God's resurrection power, they will be presented as a spotless bride, as a holy people, as those who are the workmanship of Christ. At the coming of Christ with all His saints to heaven, we will be "unblameable in holiness before God, even our Father." In that day we will not be "unblamable" because of any works on our part. It will rather reflect our entering in God's marvelous grace — unblamable because every sin is washed away, every unholy thing once and forever removed.

Sanctification the Will of God

Having held before them this glorious prospect, in Chapter 4 Paul goes on to deal with the great doctrine of sanctification: "We beseech you, brethren, and exhort you by the Lord Jesus, that as ye have received of us how ye ought to walk and to please God, so ye would abound more and more." He was never content with past spiritual achievement. There was always the appeal to be growing, expanding, having more. In verse 2 he reminds them that this is the commandment he had given them by the Lord Jesus, "For ye know what commandments we gave you by the Lord Jesus."

In verses 3-8 the great subject of sanctification is discussed. Verse 3 reads: "For this is the will of God, even your sanctification." Too often when this verse is read, those reading stop in the middle of verse 3 and do not go on to study the context. Furthermore, there is a tendency to read into this word *sanctification* the thought of moral perfection. That is not what Paul meant. What he is saying is that the Thessalonian believers were already sanctified. In other words, they had already been set apart as holy to God.

Just what does it mean to be sanctified? Suppose one were living in the time of Christ and wanted to make a gift to the temple. He would bring his gift of gold coins and lay them on the altar. What happened to those gold coins? The moment they were given to God they became sanctified. They were set apart for holy use. The sanctification did not change the character of the gold coins, but it did change their use and the purpose for which they were directed. So, every true Christian has been set apart as holy to God, even though he falls short of perfection.

SANCTIFICATION IS NOT A STATE OF SINLESSNESS

Even a casual study of the Bible will show that holiness in the Bible does not necessarily mean moral perfection. For instance, consider the expression that is found in 2 Peter, that holy men of God spoke as they were moved by the Holy Spirit. Of whom is this speaking? Peter was referring to the Old Testament writers of Scripture and to prophets who spoke the Word of God. Were those men holy? Yes, they were. The Scripture says so. Were those men perfect? Certainly not. Was Moses perfect? Was David perfect? Yet Moses wrote the law and David wrote some of the most beautiful psalms. They were not perfect, but were nevertheless holy. God had set apart these prophets to His own holy use. Though they were not perfect, He guided them so that they wrote perfect Scripture. The Word of God as it came forth from them was inspired of God. But they were still imperfect and had to strive just as we do for holy living.

SANCTIFICATION IS PRACTICAL RIGHTEOUSNESS

Does this mean Christians should not strive for holiness? Certainly not. As Paul deals with these Thessalonians he says to them: "This is the will of God, even your sanctification, that ye should abstain from fornication." The idol worship from which some of these Thessalonians had been saved included the most abominable and immoral rites. The Thessalonian Christians who were Gentiles had come out of that background, where immorality and religion were all mixed up. There is no holiness in heathen religion. Holiness was an entirely new idea. For the first time they were faced with the fact that worshiping God involved a holy life. Paul had to deal with them as he did with the Corinthians and others, reminding them that as Christians their bodies were set apart as holy to God.

In keeping with the high moral standards befitting Christians, Paul exhorts them not to give themselves to the lust of desire as the Gentiles do. In verse 6 he writes: "That no man go beyond and defraud his brother in any matter." He has in mind here a man running off with another's wife. He forbids this, because God "is the avenger of all such." In verses 7 and 8 Paul adds: "God hath not called us unto uncleanness, but unto holiness. He therefore that despiseth, despiseth not man, but God, who hath also given unto us his holy Spirit." Once again we are reminded that our bodies are the temple of the Holy Spirit and therefore we are set apart as holy to God. How we need to enter into this! Do we realize that our lives have been bought by the precious blood of Christ? Do we realize that our bodies are a holy temple occupied by the Holy Spirit? That is true whether we recognize it or not. Paul is appealing to the Thessalonian believers to live a life of holiness, a life of being set apart to the holy things of God.

CHRISTIAN LOVE IS HOLY

In verses 9 and 10 Christian love is introduced in contrast to lust. What a difference! He tells them: "But as touching brotherly love [which ought to characterize the Christian] ye need not that I write unto you: for ye yourselves are taught of God to love one another. And indeed ye do it toward all the brethren which are in all Macedonia: but we beseech you, brethren, that ye increase more and more." Love is a growing experience. We should increase more and more in our love. Do we love the Lord Jesus Christ more today than we did a year ago, or two years ago, or three years ago? We ought to. If we have been going on with the Lord we know more about Him, and the more we know about Him the more we are going to love Him. If we do not love the Lord Jesus it is because we are not very well acquainted with Him. He is altogether lovely.

WALKING HONESTLY

In verses 11 and 12 there is a very practical admonition: "That ye study to be quiet, and to do your own business, and to work with your own hands, as we commanded you; that ye may walk honestly toward them that are without, and that ye may have lack of nothing." These are words of sound wisdom. Sometimes Christians get so concerned with the coming of the Lord that they forget that there is a task to do right now.

Paul is a very practical man. He believed in the glory to come, but he also believed that we should lead a practical life. One of the things he commands is to study to be quiet. God honors the person who is quiet, particularly about his own exploits. We are exhorted also to mind our own business. No one gets into trouble minding his *own* business, but if he starts minding someone else's business, that usually causes a lot of trouble. They were exhorted to mind their own business, and to work with their own hands. Honest toil is a good thing, and God's people need to work to earn an honest living.

There are many illustrations of this in the Bible. It is recorded of Haggai and Zechariah, the great prophets who exhorted Israel to build the temple, that they worked with their own hands. When Paul ministered the gospel and ran out of funds, he did not wring his hands and say, "Now God has not been faithful to me." Oh no! He made some tents. He worked with his own hands. That is perfectly honorable. Today the standard too often is to do as little as one can for as much as one can. The Bible standard is just the opposite. The purpose of it is "That ye may walk honestly," in other words, pay our debts. Sometimes Christians are not too careful in their business relationships.

THE CALL TO HOLY LIVING

This business of sanctification, this call to holiness, extends to every aspect of our life. May God challenge us. We have been sanctified by the blood of Christ, by the power and presence of the Holy Spirit, by the purposes of God in our life in time and eternity. May we give ourselves to these things as the Holy Spirit speaks to our hearts.

Questions

1. Whom did Paul send to Thessalonica and what report did he receive from him?
2. How did Paul's response to this report indicate his great heart?
3. What was Paul's prayer for the Thessalonians?
4. What does Paul teach about sinless perfection now and in the future?
5. On what prophetic note does Chapter 3 end?
6. What three important words are used for the Lord's coming?
7. What is meant by sanctification?
8. What is the difference between love and lust?
9. What practical advice does Paul give in verses 11 and 12?

CHAPTER 4

The Translation of the Church

FIRST THESSALONIANS 4:13-18

THE DAILY EXPECTATION OF THE EARLY CHURCH

The fourth chapter of 1 Thessalonians contains one of the outstanding prophetic or eschatological passages of the New Testament. In this epistle there is constant reference to future things, each chapter closing with some allusion to prophecy. It was typical of the early church to have daily expectation that Christ would return. None of the apostles or early Christians, however, realized that the church age in which we find ourselves would be extended two thousand years. They, of course, did not set any date for the return of the Lord, but they were looking for Christ's coming in their lifetime, and this expectation continued in the early church fathers.

In the Old Testament there had been many predictions concerning Christ's coming, including His first as well as His second coming. As far as the Old Testament revelation was concerned, both comings were seen in one picture. The disciples did not understand the distinction between the two comings because the Old Testament does not make clear that there was to be a period of time between the first and the second coming of Christ. The disciples anticipated that when Christ came the first time He would fulfill the prophecies that actually pertained to His second coming, such as the earthly reign of Christ, the kingdom of righteousness and peace, and the deliverance of the Jews from their enemies, the Romans. They confidently expected that Christ would reign and that they would reign with Him. That is why they were so disappointed and disillusioned when Christ began to tell them that it was necessary for Him to die. They could not fit this into the picture. They thought Christ was going to bring in the Messianic kingdom immediately.

DOCTRINE OF TRANSLATION INTRODUCED IN JOHN 14

In Chapter 14 of John, in the very shadow of the cross, Christ reveals an amazing new revelation which He had not tried to teach them before, that is, that there was another purpose of God to be fulfilled first before bringing in the millennial kingdom. Christ told the disciples that He was going to leave them and go to heaven, that He would prepare a place for them in heaven, and that He would come back to receive them unto Himself. In other words, He revealed to them that before He fulfilled His purpose to bring in a kingdom on earth He was going to take them home to glory first. He would come back for them and take them to dwell with Him in the Father's house in heaven before His return to the earth. This truth, of course, was not completely understood by the early Christians, just as it is not completely understood by many Christians today, but it inspired a daily expectancy of His return. They were looking for Christ to come and take them home to glory. This was not death, though of course when a Christian dies we believe that he is "absent from the body" and "present with the Lord." They were looking for Christ to come and take them home to glory without dying.

THE ORDER OF RESURRECTION AND TRANSLATION

Though Paul had been in Thessalonica a short time, it is quite clear that he taught the Thessalonian Christians this truth. As this epistle makes plain, they had no doubt as to the truth of the coming of Christ for them. But there was a problem which Paul had not made clear to them. That was the question concerning the *time* when their loved ones who had died in Christ would be raised. It is evident that Paul had taught them that there would be a number of resurrections in a chronological order as the Scriptures portray — not just one general resurrection as some believe today. The question in their minds was: When, in the order of the various resurrections, would the loved ones in Christ be raised? Apparently they thought they would be caught up to be with the Lord at any time and that the resurrection of their loved ones would be delayed, possibly until after the great tribulation when Christ came back to establish His kingdom. They wanted some instruction on this point. Paul writes this letter to answer this question.

THE CERTAINTY OF CHRISTIAN HOPE

In 1 Thessalonians 4:13 Paul states: "I would not have you to be ignorant, brethren, concerning them which are asleep, that ye sorrow not, even as others which have no hope." One of the great facts of the Christian faith is that we have hope when our loved ones in Christ are taken away from us in death. Christians often fail to realize the hopelessness that characterizes heathen religions. There is no hope in the future life apart from the Lord Jesus Christ. A Christian has a wonderful hope that after this life there is going to be a glorious, unending existence in the presence of God with all the joy and ecstasy that will be ours when we are joined to Christ and with our loved ones in Christ who have gone on before us. So Paul tells the Thessalonians that he does not want them to have the attitude of the pagan world which has no hope, but instead he wants them to enter experimentally into the glory of the hope that is before them.

In verse 14 the ground for that hope is given. How certain is our hope? "For if we believe that Jesus died and rose again, even so them also which sleep in Jesus will God bring with him." In other words, the precious truth concerning the coming of Christ for His own is as certain as the central doctrine of the death and resurrection of Christ. Unless we are absolutely certain concerning the death and resurrection of Christ, we are not certain in our Christian hope. The place to begin is at the cross of Christ. It is there that Christ died for our sins; it is there we learn that we had a substitute — one who was able to save us and one who provided a sufficient sacrifice for our sin. We do not progress in our Christian faith until we come to the cross. Linked with the cross is the resurrection of Christ which is God's seal and the evidence or the apologetic for our Christian faith. Here is the stamp of certainty: Christ rose from the dead. If we believe that Christ died for us, if we believe that Christ rose from the dead, and really believe it by receiving Jesus Christ as our Savior, then we have a ground for hope.

LOVING HIS APPEARING

One of the reasons why so many in these days do not consider seriously the coming of Christ for them is that they have not been at the cross of Christ enough. Pulpits that do not proclaim the death of Christ and His resurrection can hardly be expected to preach the coming of the Lord. It is all tied together. If we accept what the Scriptures teach about the first coming of Christ and put our trust in Him, then there will be planted in our hearts an earnest desire to see the Savior, and the truth of His coming for us will be exceedingly precious. Do we really love the Lord's appearing? Does it mean anything that Christ might come back today? There are many Christians who may have it as a part of their creed, but not as a living expectation. The difficulty is that their hearts and minds are not really fixed on Christ. We will love the appearing of the Lord in direct proportion as we love the Lord Himself. If we love Him, if we long to see Him who first loved us, then the truth of the Lord's coming and the fact that He could come today will be a precious truth.

THEM WHICH ARE ASLEEP

In verse 14 there is the statement: "Them also which sleep in Jesus will God bring with him." Reference is made in verse 13 and in verse 15 to "them which are asleep," and in verse 14 to them "which sleep in Jesus." What does it mean? Sleep is a softened expression for death, which for a Christian is very much like sleep. We understand from Scripture that it refers to bodies which are laid in the grave. As far as our souls and spirits are concerned, we go immediately into the presence of God, into the conscious enjoyment of heaven, for "to be absent from the body" is "to be present with the Lord." We believe in the sleep of the body, but we do not believe in the sleep of the soul. Those whose bodies are sleeping in the grave, according to this Scripture, will be resurrected when Christ comes back.

There is a problem in verse 14 in the statement, "them also which sleep in Jesus." Literally, it is "them also which sleep through Jesus," the preposition being not *in* according to the Greek New Testament, but *through*. What does it mean to sleep through Jesus? The meaning is that when a Christian dies, his hope of being in the presence of God is made possible through Jesus. Our loved ones who are asleep through Jesus go to sleep in the certain hope of waking. Some have taken the expression "through Jesus" to go with "shall God bring with him." This is also true and may be the meaning of the expression. All our hope is certainly "through Jesus."

THE TIME OF THE RESURRECTION

In verse 15 and following Paul answers their main question. This question was not "Is the Lord coming?" or "Are we going to be with the Lord?" They believed that. The question was: "What is going to happen to our loved ones who have preceded us in death?" Some of the Thessalonians may have died a martyr's death. The expression "asleep through Jesus" could mean this. In any case, in the few months since Paul had been in Thessalonica these had slipped away from their mortal bodies. It reminds us of the uncertainty of life. Whether we are young or old, whether well or in poor health, we do not know how much time God is going to give us to serve Him in this world. These few in the Thessalonian church who had already died in Christ were illustrations of the uncertainty of human life. We should be living every day in such a way that if it is our last day on earth it will be a day well spent in the Master's will.

Because some had gone on to be with the Lord, Paul writes the Thessalonians in verses 15 and 16: "For this we say unto you by the word of the Lord, that we which are alive and remain unto the coming of the Lord shall not prevent [or "shall not precede"] them which are asleep. For the Lord himself shall descend from heaven with a shout, with the voice of the archangel, and with the trump of God: and the dead in Christ shall rise first." The question had been asked: "When will the dead in Christ be raised?"

The answer is: "The dead in Christ will be raised before we go to see the Lord." Then it follows, verse 17: "Then we which are alive and remain shall be caught up together with them in the clouds, to meet the Lord in the air: and so shall we ever be with the Lord." This passage teaches that when Christ comes back He will come back to the atmospheric heaven. When that occurs and the other events which are pictured here, Christians whose bodies have been in the grave will be resurrected, their bodies will be transformed into resurrection bodies and they will meet the Lord in the air. All of this will take place in a split second before living Christians are translated from these bodies of flesh into resurrection, immortal, incorruptible bodies.

THE TRANSLATION OF LIVING SAINTS

The companion passage to 1 Thessalonians 4 is the revelation given in 1 Corinthians 15:51-52. Just as 1 Thessalonians 4 teaches about the dead in Christ, so 1 Corinthians 15:51-52 teaches concerning the translation of the living saints. It reveals that they will be transformed in a moment, in the twinkling of an eye, and will be given immortal, incorruptible bodies. This Corinthian passage teaches very plainly the *order* of the resurrection of Christians. It is going to occur just a moment before the translation of the church. Those rising from the grave and the church on the earth are going to be caught up to meet the Lord in the air.

The Scriptures also seem to make it very clear that when Christ comes for His own He will take them to heaven where He has gone now to prepare a place for us in the Father's house (John 14:1-3). Thereafter on the earth, while the church is in glory, will take place the great climactic event of this age — the great tribulation, and the outcalling of a great many Jews and Gentiles even in that awful time who come to trust in Christ. There will be many martyrs in this period. The climax will come when Christ returns in power and glory with the angels and with the church from heaven to set up His righteous kingdom on the earth.

THE SHOUT OF COMMAND

There are some aspects of the revelation that deserve closer study. In verse 16 it is stated that the Lord Himself shall descend from heaven with a shout. This word for *shout* is a peculiar word. It is a word for a command. It is the shout of a military officer giving a command such as "Forward, march." When Christ comes back He will give a shout of command. In Chapter 11 of John the account is given of Lazarus being raised from the dead. When Christ went to the tomb and said, "Lazarus, come forth," Lazarus came forth. Some have commented that if Christ had left off the name of Lazarus, all the dead would have come forth. Such was the authority and sovereignty of our Lord Jesus Christ. Lazarus was not resurrected in the sense that we will be. He was restored to a mortal body and in due time, as age came upon him, it can be presumed that he died a natural death and was returned to the tomb. Christians will be resurrected like the resurrection body of Christ and will have a resurrection body which will never wear out, which will never be subject to death or disease or pain, a body which will last for all eternity, suited for the glorious presence of the Lord.

THE VOICE OF THE ARCHANGEL

In attendance was the voice of the archangel, who is none other than Michael, the chief of the angels, and the special protector of Israel. He also gives a shout. The Bible does not explain why Michael gives this shout or why he should be included. The Scriptures do reveal, however, that there is a great battle going on, a battle which began in the Garden of Eden and perhaps even before, and has continued through the present age. This battle is against the forces of darkness, the forces of Satan and the wicked angels and the demons who are associated with him. This is why Paul tells us that we wrestle not with flesh and blood. This is why we need to pray without ceasing. This is why we need to come to God for protection, care, and guidance. When the archangel speaks, it is a shout of victory not only for men but a shout of victory for the angels. It is a great victory for the angels when Christ comes for His church. Even though it is a work of Christ and not the angels, the archangel rejoices and exults in the tremendous victory over the forces of evil that is occasioned by the resurrection of the church from the dead.

THE TRUMP OF GOD

Another significant expression is "the trump of God." There are many trumpets mentioned in Scripture. There were trumpets in the Old Testament at the beginning of each month. There was the feast of trumpets and countless different trumpets. In the order of march, trumpets were used. The trumpet seems, in Scripture, to be a sign of assembling, a sign of going forward, of taking a new step, of unfolding something that has not been revealed before. The sounding of the trumpet here is like the sounding of the trumpet to an army. It is the call to forward march. So in this passage there is the shout, the voice of the archangel, and the trump of God. These are three separate things, but they picture to us one grand event: the coming of Christ for His church, and the translation of the church living and dead from scenes of earth to the scenes of heaven.

Some students of Scripture have had difficulty with the trump because they find other trumps in the Bible. For instance, in the Book of Revelation there is mention of seven trumpets. These are part of the dramatic sequence of events unfolded in what Christ called the great tribulation. Revelation presents first of all seven seals. Out of the seventh seal there comes a series of events which is called the seven trumpets, and out of the seventh trumpet comes another series of events known as the seven bowls of the wrath of God or the seven vials. These picture in very graphic language in the Book of Revelation the climactic events of the great tribulation leading up to the second coming of Christ.

In 1 Corinthians 15 there is mention of the last trump and some have said:

"If this is the last trump, it must be the seventh trump of Revelation." That certainly is not true! Anyone who will study the subject of trumpets from Genesis to Revelation will find that there are many trumps. In fact, the last trump of Revelation is not the last trump in the Bible at all. At the second coming of Christ, which is after the seven bowls of wrath, there still is another trump that calls the elect, mentioned in Matthew 24:31.

Is this trump of 1 Thessalonians 4 and 1 Corinthians 15:52 the same as the seventh trump of the Revelation? What do the seven trumpets of Revelation do? Every one of them is a judgment of God upon a Christ-rejecting world. They assemble no one; they are not symbols of salvation; they are not symbols of deliverance; there are no resurrections; they are symbols of judgment upon men living in the world who have rejected the Lord Jesus Christ.

By contrast, what is the significance of the trump of 1 Thessalonians 4? It is a call addressed to the saved, to those who have trusted in the Lord Jesus Christ. It is a trumpet of deliverance, of grace, and of mercy. God is dealing with His saints only in this trump and there is absolutely no connection with judgment upon unbelievers. The only similarity is that in both cases there are trumps. Simply because there is mention of the last trump in 1 Corinthians 15 does not mean that it is the last trump in God's whole program.

At Dallas Theological Seminary there are classes regulated by a system of bells. These bells ring several times each hour. The question sometimes arises concerning what bell has been ringing. There is a series of bells: a three-minute warning bell, then the bell to start the class, another warning bell five minutes before the end of the class, and finally the last bell closing the class period. When the warning bell preceding the beginning of the class rings, someone might ask, "Is that the last bell?" The answer would be, "No, that is the first bell." A few minutes later the last bell — which is the bell that begins the class — would ring. After forty-five minutes, the warning bell near the end of the class session would ring. Someone then might ask, "Is that the first bell?" The reply of course would be, "Yes, that is the first bell." In another five minutes, the bell would ring again — the last bell for the class hour. In a few minutes the whole cycle of bells begins again for the next hour. The last bell for one class hour would ring before the first bell of the next hour. How ridiculous it would be to make all the "last bells" one and the same. So it is with the trumpets of Scripture. The last trumpet for the church is long before any of the trumpets of Revelation.

MEETING THE LORD IN THE AIR

The Thessalonians passage continues with another tremendous revelation. "The dead in Christ shall rise first: then we which are alive and remain shall be caught up together with them in the clouds, to meet the Lord in the air: and so shall we ever be with the Lord." This Scripture does not reveal where we are to go with the Lord, but, as has been already indicated, John 14 tells us plainly that when Christ comes for us He will take us to the Father's house in heaven. When we meet the Lord in the air, we shall assemble in the atmospheric heaven and from there go to the third heaven, which is the immediate presence of the Father. This is indicated in the last part of the preceding chapter where Paul speaks of our being in the presence of God the Father, unblamable in holiness.

It will be a wonderful event when you and I who have trusted in the Lord Jesus Christ in this life stand in His presence. In that triumphant moment we will be like Christ for we are told in 1 John 3 that we will be perfectly holy. We will be cleansed from every spot and wrinkle and every sign of age and corruption. We will be a perfect and a beautiful bride for our Lord and Savior Jesus Christ and shall be with Him forever. Whether Christ is in heaven or reigning on the earth, or in the new earth or the new heaven in eternity future, wherever Christ is there shall the church also be. We are going to be with the Lord forever.

THE DEAD IN CHRIST

A fascinating sideline study is the expression "the dead in Christ" (v. 16). What does it mean to be "in Christ" and who are the dead in Christ? Obviously the "dead in Christ" are those who in life were in Christ and have died a physical death. In other words, their bodies have been laid in the grave and their spirits have gone to heaven. This expression occurs about forty times in the New Testament and in most of these instances refers to our position in Christ. When a person receives Jesus Christ as Savior and trusts in Him as the Son of God, as the one who died for him on the cross and who shed His blood for his sins and rose in triumph, God does something. He saves his soul.

At the very moment God saves us many wonderful things happen. Lewis Sperry Chafer in his book *Salvation* lists thirty-three things that occur instantaneously the very moment a person puts His trust in Jesus Christ. One of the things that occurs is that we are placed in Christ which the Scriptures explain by telling us that we are baptized into one body and are baptized into Christ. We become an integral part of the organism which is the church of Jesus Christ in the world. This occurs the instant we really trust in Christ. Every genuine Christian is equally in Christ. First Thessalonians 4 teaches that the dead in Christ will be raised when Christ comes back. It is a selective resurrection. All dead will not be raised. The Scriptures make it plain that unsaved people will not be raised until many years later after the predicted millennium as is made very clear in the twentieth chapter of the Book of Revelation. The question which has bothered Bible students is whether the dead in Christ include all the saints who have died up to this point or does it include only the saints of this dispensation, that is, from the Day of Pentecost until the present time?

C. I. Scofield, who edited the *Scofield Reference Bible* which has been such a blessing to countless numbers of readers, says in a note on 1 Thessalonians 4 that the dead in Christ includes all the saints. Lewis Sperry Chafer, who was for nearly two decades Scofield's associate, after studying the question for many years came to a different conclusion, that the expression the "dead in Christ" refers only to the saints of this dispensation. If the translation occurs *before* the time of great tribulation pictured in the Bible, then the resurrection of the Old Testament saints would occur *after* the tribulation in connection with Christ's return to establish His kingdom. If two men of God like Scofield and Chafer differ, how can we determine the correct interpretation? The key seems to be in the phrase "in Christ."

This expression "in Christ" in every one of its many instances in the New Testament refers only to the saints of this dispensation. As far as the expression "the dead in Christ" indicates, only those in Christ are raised. Of course, all the saints are in Christ in the sense that Christ is their substitute, but the question is whether they are in the body of Christ, baptized into His body, as the Scriptures picture.

The doctrine of the resurrection of the Old Testament saints, as it is revealed in the Old Testament itself, relates the event to the second coming of Christ to establish His kingdom. By way of illustration, Daniel 12:1 deals with the great tribulation. Daniel 12:2 speaks of many being raised from the dust of the earth. If that is a genuine resurrection, it is a clear indication that according to Daniel the resurrection of the Old Testament saints occurs after the tribulation. The resurrection of the church, however, occurs before the tribulation. There is no explicit teaching anywhere in the Bible that reveals that the Old Testament saints are resurrected at the time the church is resurrected. In other words, the two events are never brought together in any passage of Scripture. The best explanation of the expression "dead in Christ" is to refer it to the church alone.

THE COMFORT OF THE LORD'S RETURN

The Thessalonians were having a hard time and this wonderful truth of the coming of the Lord, the resurrection of their loved ones, and their being gathered together to be with the Lord was a joyous prospect. Paul writes accordingly, "Wherefore comfort one another with these words." This is another good reason why the Lord is going to come for His church before the tribulation. Paul did not tell these Thessalonian Christians: "Now if you endure through the tribulation time, if you survive that awful period, then you will see your loved ones at the end." That would not have been an encouragement to them. They were in trouble already and no doubt they had been taught that the time of great tribulation would be much worse than the trouble they then had. Instead, Paul lifts up their eyes to contemplate the coming of the Lord and they were comforted; they were encouraged by the fact that the Lord would come at any time to receive them unto Himself.

THE CHALLENGE OF THE TRUTH

This very precious truth of the Lord's return is certainly very important and one that is most significant, but it depends on our personal relationship to Jesus Christ. Are we really trusting Him? Is our heart, our faith, our life really centered in the Lord Jesus Christ? Some Christians are actually afraid of the doctrine of the Lord's coming, and of the thought that the Lord might come today. Such an attitude is born of ignorance and unbelief. Oh the prospect, the joy of looking forward to the coming of the Lord, and of resting in these precious truths! There are so many ills of life that nothing can heal except the Lord's return. How many loved ones are on the other side and how many problems of this life, incurable diseases, pain, sorrow, difficulties will be made all right. As we face the duties and the challenges and the trials of life, God has given us this blessed hope, this hope of the Lord's return. May we take it to our bosoms, may we live in its reality, and may our hearts be refreshed by this precious truth. This hope can be the certain prospect of anyone who will trust in Jesus Christ the Son of God, who loved us and died for us, who shed His blood that we might be saved, and who rose in victory that we might have hope.

Questions

1. Where is the doctrine of the rapture first introduced in the Bible?
2. What was the problem which the Thessalonians had concerning the relationship of resurrection and translation?
3. Is there evidence that God wants believers to understand prophecy?
4. How does prophecy relate to comfort?
5. How certain is the hope of the Lord's return?
6. What does it mean that Christ will bring those "which sleep in Jesus" with Him and why does He do it?
7. What is Paul's authority for his teaching on the rapture?
8. Explain how the shout of the Lord, the voice of the archangel, and the trump of God relate to the rapture.
9. Who responds first to the command to be raptured and how does this solve the problem of the Thessalonians?
10. Where do believers meet Christ?
11. Is there any indication in Scripture where the saints will go after they meet Christ in the air?

12. What does the expression "the dead in Christ" mean?
13. In what sense is the Lord's return a comfort to the Thessalonians and to us?
14. Does Paul predict any events as preceding the rapture of the church in this passage?

CHAPTER 5

The Day of the Lord
FIRST THESSALONIANS 5:1-11

First Thessalonians 5:1-11 deals with the subject of the Day of the Lord. The Bible indicates that tremendous events are ahead for the world. Gathered under the expression "the day of the Lord" is a large group of prophetic events predicted in both the Old and the New Testaments. The subject of the translation of the church revealed in Chapter 4 of 1 Thessalonians, however, is never mentioned in the Old Testament. There is no reference in the Old Testament to saints being raptured, taken from earth to heaven without dying. There are many references to Christ coming back to the earth and of resurrection from the dead, but no rapture, no translation in the Old Testament, except by way of illustration in the cases of Elijah and Enoch.

WHAT IS THE DAY OF THE LORD?

In considering the Day of the Lord, we at once are plunged into a tremendous Old Testament doctrine, a doctrine that covers many pages in the Old Testament. Before examining the Scriptural revelation, it is necessary to determine precisely what this expression, "the day of the Lord" means. We say that the present age is the day of grace. We do not mean that there was no grace shown by God in the previous dispensations. Obviously, many of God's dealings with man from the Garden of Eden down to the present day have manifested the grace of God. But God in this present age has especially singled out the doctrine of grace for display, revealing grace as a basis for salvation and for our Christian life. Grace speaks of God's unmerited favor to us through Christ who loved us and who died for us. The Scriptures picture that after this day of grace has come to its close, which may be simultaneous with the translation of the church, the Day of the Lord will begin.

The Day of the Lord is a period of time in which God will deal with wicked men directly and dramatically in fearful judgment. Today a man may be a blasphemer of God, an atheist, can denounce God and teach bad doctrine. Seemingly God does nothing about it. But the day designated in Scripture as "the day of the Lord" is coming when God will punish human sin, and He will deal in wrath and in judgment with a Christ-rejecting world. One thing we are sure of, that God in His own way will bring every soul into judgment.

The word *day* is used in the Bible in various ways. Sometimes it is used to refer to daylight; for instance, the hours between dawn and sunset. Sometimes it is used to refer to a twenty-four hour day. The Jewish day began at sunset and continued to the next day at sunset. That also is referred to as a day. Sometimes the word *day* is used in the Bible as a period of time, just as we use it in English. We speak of the day of our youth; what do we mean by that? We do not mean that we were young only one day, but we mean the extended period of time in which we were young. In 1 Thessalonians 5 the Day of the Lord is used in the sense of an extended period of time, but having the characteristics of a twenty-four hour day. That is, it is a day which begins at midnight or in the darkness, advancing to dawn and then daylight. It will close again with another period of darkness after daylight has passed. That apparently is the symbolism involved in the Day of the Lord. A few sample passages, out of literally dozens of them in the Old Testament, will give the general content of this period.

THE DAY OF THE LORD IN THE OLD TESTAMENT

The prophecy of Isaiah 13:9-11 speaks for itself: "Behold, the day of the LORD cometh, cruel both with wrath and fierce anger, to lay the land desolate: and he shall destroy the sinners thereof out of it. For the stars of heaven and the constellations thereof shall not give their light: the sun shall be darkened in his going forth, and the moon shall not cause her light to shine. And I will punish the world for their evil, and the wicked for their iniquity; and I will cause the arrogancy of the proud to cease, and will lay low the haughtiness of the terrible." In other words, there will be a great and dramatic judgment, manifest in the physical world, which will interfere with the light of the sun, moon, and stars. God will put down the proud and deal with the sinners. It is a time of judgment.

The same thought is found in Zephaniah 1:14-16: "The great day of the LORD is near, it is near, and hasteth greatly, even the voice of the day of the LORD: the mighty man shall cry there bitterly. That day is a day of wrath, a day of trouble and distress, a day of wasteness and desolation, a day of darkness and gloominess, a day of clouds and thick darkness, a day of the trumpet and alarm against the fenced cities, and against the high towers." This passage continues in the same strain. The Day of the Lord, according to the Old Testament, is a time of God's judgment and a time of God's dealing with the world in its sin.

The Day of the Lord is also a time of deliverance and blessing for Israel. The millennium — the whole kingdom reign of Christ on earth — in which

Christ personally directs the government of the world, is also included in the Day of the LORD. In Zephaniah 3:14-15, by way of illustration, there is a picture of Israel's blessing in that day, obviously following the time of judgment: "Sing, O daughter of Zion; shout, O Israel; be glad and rejoice with all the heart, O daughter of Jerusalem. The LORD hath taken away thy judgments, he hath cast out thine enemy; the king of Israel, even the LORD, is in the midst of thee: thou shalt not see evil any more." The passage here sets forth the praise and joy and rejoicing of Israel in the millennium. The Day of the Lord, as revealed in the Old Testament, indicates first a time of wrath and judgment upon a wicked and Christ-rejecting world which is followed by a time of peace in which Christ shall be in the midst of the earth and will rule over the earth and bring blessing to the nation Israel. The millennium will end with another night of judgment (Rev. 20:9-15).

THE DAY OF WRATH

The truth concerning the coming of Christ for His church is revealed in 1 Thessalonians 4. The question which is answered in 1 Thessalonians 5 is "What relationship has the coming of Christ to the Day of the Lord?" In verse 1, accordingly, Paul writes: "But of the times and seasons, brethren, ye have no need that I write unto you." The word *time* here is a translation of the Greek word from which we get our word *chronology*. Of the time — the general chronology, and of the seasons — the particular time — he states he has no need to write unto them. In other words, they had already been instructed, first, concerning the general time when Christ would come and, second, concerning the particular time. In a word, it is this: the general time can be known, but the particular time cannot. That is the point of his message.

In verses 2 and 3 he says: "For yourselves know perfectly that the day of the Lord so cometh as a thief in the night. For when they shall say, Peace and safety; then sudden destruction cometh upon them, as travail upon a woman with child; and they shall not escape." The Day of the Lord is described as a day of wrath, which is a very important point. Compare this passage with the sixth chapter of Revelation which is about the time of the beginning of the great tribulation. This portion of Scripture is also similar to what Isaiah and Zephaniah said about the day of judgment in the Day of the Lord. Is not this the same period?

Revelation 6:12-14 states: "And I beheld when he had opened the sixth seal, and, lo, there was a great earthquake, and the sun became black as sackcloth of hair, and the moon became as blood, and the stars of heaven fell unto the earth, even as a fig tree casteth her untimely figs, when she is shaken of a mighty wind. And the heaven departed as a scroll when it is rolled together, and every mountain and island were moved out of their places."

This is exactly the same thought and is also a warning of judgment upon men.

In Revelation 6:16-17 we learn that the wicked cry out and say "to the mountains and rocks, Fall on us, and hide us from the face of him that sitteth on the throne, and from the wrath of the Lamb. For the great day of his wrath is come; and who shall be able to stand?" Isaiah said it was a day of wrath; Zephaniah said it was a day of wrath; Revelation 6 says it is a day of wrath. In other words, the picture we have here of the great tribulation — the time of trouble on the earth — is identical to the picture of the Old Testament revelation of the beginning of the Day of the Lord.

RELATION TO COMING OF THE LORD

The question is: "How does the coming of Christ for His church relate itself to the Day of the Lord which precedes the second coming of Christ by a number of years?" This Day of the Lord will come suddenly and unexpectedly. What is the point? The point is that just as the translation of the church is the end of the day of grace it also marks the beginning of the Day of the Lord. In other words, the one event seems to do two things: it serves as the closing of one day and the beginning of the other. If that is true, it gives us some very positive and definite teaching along the line that the church will be taken out of the world before the day of trial and trouble overtakes the world. Paul is telling the Thessalonians that the Day of the Lord is going to come, and this follows immediately the passage which dealt with the coming of Christ for His church. In 1 Thessalonians 5 it is revealed that the Day of the Lord comes suddenly and unexpectedly. It is described: "the day of the Lord so cometh as a thief in the night." A thief in the night comes unheralded. There are no signs that pertain to a thief.

UNEXPECTED BY THE WORLD

The judgment will come when the world is expecting peace and safety — just the opposite of the time of trouble which is predicted. At the time of the beginning of the Day of the Lord there will be some evidence for peace. Apparently the world situation at the beginning of the Day of the Lord will provide a false basis for peace. This may be accomplished by a strengthened "United Nations" or world organization. This state of peace is quite in contrast, however, to the revealed situation at the second coming. Then the armies of the world will be drawn in battle array at Armageddon. The world will be engaged in a gigantic military struggle then. But at the beginning of the Day of the Lord they will be saying "Peace and safety." In that very time sudden destruction comes. In the Greek New Testament the word *sudden* is emphasized. That event will not be preceded by signs, that is, there will be no warning. There will be no possibility of escape. The illustration given is that of travail coming suddenly upon a woman with child. It will be God's divine, unescapable judgment upon those who are "in darkness." The beginning of the Day of the Lord is clearly not the second coming of Christ. It is rather begun much before this and may begin at once when the day of grace closes with the translation of the church.

DAY OF THE LORD DOES NOT OVERTAKE CHRISTIANS

How are Christians related to this judgment? Verse 4 states: "But ye, brethren, are not in darkness, that that day should overtake you as a thief." Christians, of course, do not know when the Day of the Lord is coming either. As far as expectation is concerned, they are in the dark about it. Christ could come today and the Day of the Lord would follow, but no one can set the day. It is unexpected in this sense for us. What does He mean then by the statement, "ye . . . are not in darkness, that that day should overtake you as a thief"?

The best explanation is that we will not be here. When the Day of the Lord comes, we will be in glory. "Ye, brethren, are not in darkness, that that day should overtake you as a thief. Ye are all the children of light, and the children of the day: we are not of the night, nor of darkness." In other words, we belong to a different dispensation, to a different day. We belong to the day of grace. Why should a child of God's grace — who is saved by grace, who is kept by grace, who has all the wonderful promises of God — be forced to go through a period which according to Scripture is expressly designed as a time of judgment upon a Christ-rejecting world? We belong to the day; they belong to the night. The passage continues: "Ye are all the children of light, and the children of the day: we are not of the night, nor of darkness."

APPLICATION OF THE TRUTH

In verse 5 the doctrinal section is brought to its close. Verses 1-5 have revealed that the Day of the Lord will come suddenly as a destruction upon the wicked, but we as Christians will have no part in it because we do not belong to that period of time. In verses 6-11 Paul makes the application. All true prophetic teaching has an application. The study of prophecy is not just for prophecy's sake. God has taught us concerning future things because He wants us to be informed and, being informed, to be better Christians. One of the reasons for presenting the doctrine of the imminent return of Christ is that it is an impelling motive to be living for Him every day. There is no better reason for working for Christ, apart from real love for Him, than the motive that we may see Him today. It makes a tremendous difference whether Christ is coming now or whether our prospect is that we will go through the tribulation and our only hope of seeing Him without dying would be to go through that awful time of trouble. The imminency of the Lord's return is a precious truth.

On the basis of this hope an exhortation is given, based upon the imminency of the Lord's return: "Therefore let us not sleep, as do others; but let us watch and be sober." The word *sober* in the original means exactly what is meant by it in English. It is the word for not being intoxicated. We are so prone to be intoxicated, not necessarily by liquor but by the stimulants of the world — its glamour, pleasures, and appearance. Paul's message to these Thessalonian Christians reveals also that we should be watching for the coming of the Lord. If we realize the solemnity of the event for us and for those who will be left behind, how earnestly it should make us watch and be sober! How we should be diligent in our Christian life and profession because of the imminent coming of Christ!

FAITH, HOPE, LOVE

Paul goes on to plead his case: "They that sleep sleep in the night; and they that be drunken are drunken in the night." That is the world's life. "But let us, who are of the day, be sober, putting on the breastplate of faith and love; and for an helmet, the hope of salvation." In Chapter 1 mention was made of these same three things — faith, love, and hope. In 1:3 Paul reminds the Thessalonians of their labor of love, and their work of faith, and patience of hope. In 1 Corinthians, Chapter 13, the same triad is found — faith, hope, and love. On the basis of our being "of the day," we are to go on in the faith for the Lord. We are to put on the breastplate of faith and love, the best possible protection for spiritual battles. In addition, we should put on "for an helmet, the hope of salvation."

NOT APPOINTED TO WRATH

In verse 9 it is stated: "For God hath not appointed us to wrath, but to obtain salvation by our Lord Jesus Christ." In this passage he is expressly saying that our appointment is to be caught up to be with Christ; the appointment of the world is for the Day of the Lord, the day of wrath. One cannot keep both of these appointments. Certainly, there will be some after the church is gone who will turn to Christ, and in Revelation 7 it is stated that there will be an innumerable company of martyrs. Many will be saved after the church has gone to heaven, but they will experience the awfulness of that period. As the wrath of God is poured upon the earth, it will involve them too.

When an atom bomb explodes over a city in the tribulation, it will kill believers as well as those who are not. They will participate in the awful trials and troubles of that day, and the reason they will be subjected to these things is that they were not ready for Christ when He came for His church.

They had not trusted in the Lord Jesus Christ at that time. But you and I who have trusted Him, who have believed in Christ as our personal Savior, are not appointed to that day of wrath. We are appointed unto the day of grace to meet Christ in the air and to be forever with the Lord. This passage of Scripture teaches that Christ is coming for His church *before* the Day of the Lord begins, *before* the day of trouble pictured in Revelation and all through the Bible overtakes the world. We are not appointed to wrath, but to salvation.

APPOINTED TO SALVATION

The passage explains the basis for this. In that day, in connection with our faith in Christ, we will have obtained "salvation by our Lord Jesus Christ, who died for us, that, whether we wake or sleep, we should live together with him. Wherefore, comfort yourselves together, and edify one another, even as also ye do." In other words, whether we "wake," that is, are living in the world at the time the Lord comes, or whether we "sleep" and our bodies have been laid in the grave, though our spirits have gone to heaven, when Christ comes back for His church there will be a wonderful reunion — both a translation of the living saints and a resurrection from the dead. It is all based on the hope of the death of Christ. Some think that only very spiritual Christians are going to be raptured, including of course those who hold this theory. Most of us would like to meet some of these specially spiritual folks. We may know many very fine Christians, but have we ever found one yet who was perfect? No, not yet. If our being translated depended upon our perfection, all of us would be required to go through the tribulation. If, on the other hand, our being raptured depends on the death and the resurrection of Christ as this picture indicates, then every true believer in Christ who has trusted in Him as his sacrifice for sin and as his God and his Savior will be translated when Christ comes and will go home to glory with the Lord and with the loved ones who have gone on before.

THE EXHORTATION

On the basis of this wonderful prospect, we should "comfort" one another and encourage one another in the faith, "even as also ye do." As we look forward to the coming of the Lord, may it not only be a part of our theology and of our hope, but may it be the mainspring of our Christian life and testimony. If today is the last day on earth before Christ comes, may it be a day that is well spent in God's service for His glory and for the testimony of the truth!

Questions

1. What is the meaning of the expression "the day of the Lord"?
2. To what extent is the Day of the Lord a day of wrath?
3. How does the Day of the Lord relate to the rapture?
4. Why does the Day of the Lord overtake the world as a surprise but does not overtake Christians as a surprise?
5. What exhortations does Paul give on the basis of the truth of the coming of the Day of the Lord?
6. Relate the words faith, love, and hope in Chapter 5 with Chapter 1.
7. How do you explain that Christians are not appointed to wrath and how does this relate to the question of whether Christians will be on earth during the Day of the Lord?
8. How does Paul relate to our comfort the fact that Christians will not enter the Day of the Lord?

CHAPTER 6

Christian Testimony in the Light of the Lord's Return

FIRST THESSALONIANS 5:12-28

TESTIMONY TOWARD CHRISTIAN LEADERS

While First Thessalonians unfolds many great doctrinal revelations, it closes with a very practical note. First, the general theme of our testimony is presented. What do others see in our Christian life? In verses 12-13 the rather unusual point of view is presented concerning our testimony toward those who are our spiritual leaders. Paul exhorts them in these verses: "We beseech you, brethren, to know them which labour among you, and over you in the Lord, and admonish you; and to esteem them very highly in love for their work's sake. And be at peace among yourselves."

There was an unusual situation in this church at Thessalonica, arising from the fact that the church had been in existence only a few months. Every member of this church was a new convert. Some of them had probably been saved on the same day, or in the same week. God had taken this church and had called out a few of their number to be leaders. They had not had any seminary or college or Bible institute training. All they had was what Paul had given them and what the Spirit of God had taught them in the days and weeks which followed. But God had put His hand upon some to be teachers and leaders, and some overseers of God's people. Paul's message to this Thessalonian church is, "Give recognition to those who have the gift of leadership."

It is naturally difficult for two Christians who start out the same way and have come from the same background to recognize that one is better than the other as far as administering the Lord's work is concerned. Some may have said of a leader, "Who is he to take the place of leadership in the church?" Paul is telling them to recognize people according to their ministry, not for what they are, but for what they are doing as ministers of the Lord. Thus Paul writes: "I ask you," or "beseech you, brethren, to know them which labour among you" — to know them in the sense of respecting them. He refers to the leaders as those "who are over you in the Lord."

Christians are all alike in the sense that both the clergy and laity are on the same level. But the Bible also teaches that we do not all have the same gifts.

57

Some can teach; some can administer; some can help; some can pray. There is a difference in the opportunity and the way in which we serve the Lord. If a believer has gifts of teaching and of being a leader, other members in the church should recognize that and respond to these gifts and the exercise of them which God has given. The Thessalonians were exhorted to do this, and to accept the admonition given to them by those who teach.

In verse 13 Paul exhorts, "to esteem them very highly in love for their work's sake." How carefully Paul expresses it! He does not say: "Accept them because they are unusually fine looking, or because they are well dressed, or because they have such fine gifts of oratory." There were many things, no doubt, that were commendable about those leaders, but that was not the point. They should be esteemed because of the work they were doing. In other words, when we recognize that God is using a man, it is in the end a recognition of God and His sovereign choice, of divine grace and gifts, and not of the man himself. The glory must remain with God even though we recognize the instrument. We are to esteem them highly for their work's sake. While God expects us to be discerning and not to accept that which is contrary to the Word of God, any criticism should be in love and for the furtherance of the work of God. We are very definitely taught that we should esteem God's servants, even the humble ones, very highly for their work's sake.

Then Paul adds, "And be at peace among yourselves." The relationship of recognizing leadership to peace is a very obvious one. It is impossible for any work of God to be run by everyone. There must be someone who is responsible for different parts. It is possible to have too many cooks in the kitchen. That is also true in the work of the Lord. We can have too many people trying to run the church. We should recognize leaders and pray for them, at the same time being willing to follow the leadership that is given. Peace among ourselves requires also that each person do his own work and not the work of someone else, responding to the plan and program as God has led in it.

TESTIMONY TO CHRISTIAN BRETHREN

In verses 14-15 our testimony toward our Christian brother is discussed. Paul encourages them and commands, "Brethren, warn them that are unruly." The word used here for *warn* is the same word used in verse 12 for *admonish*. It is the idea of warning in a sense of instructing or admonishing them, encouraging them to do that which is right. We are to admonish those who are unruly, who are not cooperating in the work of the Lord, who are doing the wrong thing. Apparently they had trouble even in that day with people who did not get in line and do the thing they ought to do. Then Paul also told them to "comfort the feebleminded," as we have it in the Authorized Version, or, better translated, "to comfort the feeble in spirit," or "the weak spirited." There are some who are discouraged very easily. Perhaps they have an inferiority complex and they need much encouragement. All of us have had the experience in life of being very discouraged at times and when someone spoke an encouraging word it helped us a great deal.

We are also to support the weak. The weak here apparently refers to weakness in our spiritual life. Some Christians are just weak, that is, they are easily led astray. They have not learned to lean upon Christ to support them, and to help and encourage them. In this church of young Christians, they were exhorted by Paul to support the weak and at the same time commanded to "be patient toward all men." While some must have specialized treatment when it comes to patience, there is not a Christian living who does not need to have a little patience administered to him at times. Do not expect anyone to be perfect, but have a little patience whenever it is required. "Be patient toward all."

In verse 15 a great Christian principle is stated: "See that none render evil for evil unto any man; but ever follow that which is good, both among yourselves, and to all men." Someone has said that there are three standards: first, the standard of the heathen wicked world which does evil in response to good; second, there is the attitude of the so-called cultured world which is to do good toward those who do good to them; third, there is the attitude of Christian faith to do good to them who do evil to us. This is contrary to the natural man; it is contrary to natural ethics, but it is according to the Word of God. The Thessalonian Christians are admonished here not to pay back evil for evil, not to try to get even, not to take things into their own hands. They were being persecuted for their faith and were having a hard time. How easy it would have been for them to "get even," as we say. But Paul said, No, that is not the Christian way. The Christian way is to take evil and respond with good. Certainly that is what God has done for us. God has surely shown His love particularly for those who have trusted in Christ. God has taken the evil which resulted in the crucifixion of Christ, and in response to our sins God has done us good. He has given us grace and salvation. He has given us hope in the Lord Jesus.

Our Testimony Toward God

In verses 16-23 the third aspect of our testimony is presented, our testimony toward God. Our testimony toward those who minister over us was considered in verses 12-13, and our testimony toward our Christian brethren was discussed in verses 14-15. Now the most important of all — our testimony before God — is examined. The world can see only our outer life, but God really knows what we are doing. He knows our hearts, our attitude, and the real character of our spiritual life. Paul raises the ultimate question of all, "What does God think about us?" In answer to that question, he gives the most simple and yet profound exhortation to be found anywhere in the Word.

In verses 16-18 three exhortations are grouped together. It is not as clear in the English as it is in the Greek New Testament. In verse 18 it begins, "This is the will of God in Christ Jesus concerning you," and it seems clear from the Greek that these three commands — "rejoice," "pray," and "give thanks" — are summed up as a unit, as combining the will of God. Here is Christian testimony in relation to God in a very concise statement. What are these three things?

REJOICE EVERMORE

First, in verse 16 the command is given, "Rejoice evermore." This verse is the shortest verse in the Bible. Some think that "Jesus wept" (John 11:35) is the shortest, and in the English it is. In the New Testament in Greek, 1 Thessalonians 5:16 is the shortest verse in the Bible. It contains two words and they are short words, whereas in the original for "Jesus wept" there are three words and they are longer words. Even though it is the shortest verse in the Bible, it certainly says a great deal.

One of the amazing things about the Word of God is that it can say so much in a few words. Suppose that all that was known about a Christian was that he rejoiced evermore. How much would you know? You could be sure that he was genuinely saved. The world may have its pleasure, but it knows nothing of rejoicing evermore. For the Christian who is living in the will of God, there is the possibility of rejoicing evermore. It shows that a person is living in the realm of faith, trusting the Lord. Does that characterize our lives as God knows our lives? Consider the simple sin of murmuring as recorded in the Book of Exodus and other books which tell of Israel's journey from Egypt to the promised land. God punished them severely for their murmuring. They complained about the same things which we are apt to complain about: our food, our drink, our circumstances. Here we have the opposite to murmuring, that Christians should rejoice evermore.

PRAY WITHOUT CEASING

The next verse is, "Pray without ceasing." What does it mean to pray without ceasing? Does it mean to stay on one's knees twenty-four hours a day? No, our Lord did not do that, and Paul did not either. Then, what does he mean by praying without ceasing? It means, first of all, that Paul maintained his stated times of prayer. Daniel prayed three times a day. When the decree was given that he should not do it, what did he do? Did he stop? Did he cut out one of them? Or did he close the windows? No, he went right on faithfully, three times a day. He continued in prayer without ceasing. He went right on praying at his stated times. It represents the fact also that we are always in touch with God. Certainly two friends can be in the same room and be in harmony and fellowship one with the other, even though they may not be talking with each other all the time. Paul is saying, "Do you want a really rich experience? Begin a walk of fellowship with the Lord, not only at stated times of prayer, in which you bring all your needs to the Lord, but also the unbroken walk of communion — praying without ceasing."

In Everything Give Thanks

In verse 18 Paul adds the third exhortation, "In everything give thanks." Put these three things together. "Rejoice evermore. Pray without ceasing. In every thing give thanks." There is no easier or a more simple recipe for a happy Christian experience. What does it mean, "In every thing give thanks"? It does not necessarily mean *for* everything give thanks. It means this: that in every circumstance of life, no matter where God puts you, no matter what your difficulties are, in those circumstances you can thank God for all He has done for you. You may be praying earnestly that He will change your circumstances. You may be praying for victory. You can thank God that in it all you will be victorious in Christ. So in everything give thanks. This recipe, of course, is the will of God, as we have it stated so plainly here, "this is the will of God in Christ Jesus concerning you."

Quench Not the Spirit

In verses 19-22 there is a further admonition. These four verses relate to the first command of this section, "Quench not the Spirit." This tremendous doctrine in a word is this: When Christ went to heaven He sent the Holy Spirit. On the Day of Pentecost every true believer in Christ was indwelt by the Spirit. Ever since, whenever a person really trusts in Christ as his Savior, the Holy Spirit comes into his mortal body and makes it a holy sanctuary, a temple of God. The Holy Spirit is there to minister to us. He is there to teach us, to guide us, to direct us, to rebuke us, to show us the way to unfold the Scripture, to give us joy and peace and love, and to transform our lives and our character and our experience. How manifold are the ministries of the Holy Spirit! Yet, you and I have within us under the providence of God the capacity to quench or stifle the Spirit. Sometimes we see Christians who we know are saved, but their lives do not reflect the fragrance of the presence of God. What is wrong with them? They are resisting the Holy Spirit. What is it to quench the Spirit? It is just saying "no" to God. We should instead always be saying, "Yes, Lord."

In thus yielding to the Lord, the Thessalonian Christians were told they should, first of all, not despise prophesyings. Further, they were to "prove all things; hold fast that which is good." In other words, everything they heard was not necessarily prophesied. They had to distinguish between truth and error, even as we do today. They had to hold to what was good and put away that which was bad. In verse 22 Paul summed up what it means to quench not the Spirit, "Abstain from all appearance of evil," or, as it is better translated, "Abstain from every form of evil." We have the broad statement that regardless of what it is in our life that may be contrary to the will of God, it should be taken out of our life.

COMPLETE SANCTIFICATION

In verse 23, in conclusion, Paul contemplates the time when we are going to be perfect in the presence of God. In a word, it is the truth that God has set us apart to holy living. It does not mean that we are perfect now. Paul was not perfect; John was not perfect. It does mean that we should be holy, belonging to the Lord. "The very God of peace sanctify you wholly," that is, in every respect. He continues, May "your whole spirit and soul and body be preserved blameless unto the coming of our Lord Jesus Christ." The word *whole* here refers to the parts of our natural life: our spirit, our soul, and our body. Each of these three parts should be preserved holy to God and be used by God. That means that everything we are belongs to the Lord — our physical bodies, our spiritual or intellectual life, and our psychological or natural life.

In verse 24 Paul reminds us, "Faithful is he that calleth you, who also will do it." No one can sanctify himself. God has to set us apart as holy to Himself, and the great truth here is, "Faithful is he who is going to do this."

Verse 25 is a very understandable exhortation. Paul writes: "Brethren, pray for us." We need prayer. It takes prayer and the work of the Holy Spirit to accomplish any true work for God. After this appeal, Paul closes with a greeting to all the brethren. He charges them to have the epistle read. He was conscious of the fact that this was the very Word of God. Finally, he concludes with that great benediction: "The grace of our Lord Jesus Christ be with you. Amen." As Paul wrote this to the Thessalonian Christians, so may the grace of God, His favor, His enablement, be made real in all our lives.

Questions

1. What should be the relationship of Christians to Christian leaders and how does this relate particularly to the Thessalonian church?
2. What should characterize our testimony toward our Christian brethren?
3. What should characterize our testimony toward God?
4. What should characterize our rejoicing, prayer, and giving of thanks?

5. What is meant by the command: "Quench not the Spirit" and what does Paul include as evidence of it?
6. What does Paul mean by his prayer that God will "sanctify you wholly"?
7. Who does the sanctifying?
8. What is Paul's final request?

CHAPTER 7

Glorifying God in Tribulation
SECOND THESSALONIANS 1:1-12

OCCASION OF THE EPISTLE

The Second Epistle of Paul to the Thessalonians followed the first epistle by a relatively short time of a few months. Its occasion was the receipt of the news that the Thessalonians had received a spurious letter, apparently an intentional forgery, teaching them that they were already in the Day of the Lord and its awful judgments. The background of both the Thessalonian epistles indicates that the church was going through a terrible time of persecution. In the midst of these trials, they began to wonder whether they were in the Day of the Lord, a period described at great length in the Old Testament and concerning which Paul had taught them in 1 Thessalonians. The beginning of this period of tremendous trouble and conflict in the world is identified with the great judgments which are poured out on the world before the second coming of Christ. The Thessalonians, on the basis of the forged letter, wondered whether they were in this time of trouble, in contradiction to Paul's teaching that the church would be translated before the Day of the Lord began (1 Thess. 5). Paul is, accordingly, writing this letter to straighten out their misunderstanding. Paul's answer, in a word, is that this predicted time of trouble which begins the Day of the Lord was still future. The persecutions they were undergoing were the normal persecutions that can be experienced by all Christians throughout the church age.

SALUTATION

The second epistle opens with a salutation practically word for word the same as the first epistle. Silas, called here Silvanus, and Timothy, called Timotheus, join Paul in this letter. These three had brought the gospel to the Thessalonians and so together they send their greetings. As in the first epistle, the church is declared to be "in God our Father and the Lord Jesus Christ" (v. 1). Though their earthly circumstance was one of great trial and affliction, their position before God, like all other believers, was in Christ and in God the Father. It is a marvelous truth that we as Christians have the same position in Christ regardless of circumstances, whether affliction or joy

64

be our portion. The fact that we are in Christ continues unchanged all through our life and will continue through eternity.

APOSTOLIC GREETING

In verse 2 the apostolic greeting is repeated, "Grace unto you, and peace, from God our Father and the Lord Jesus Christ." In our English version most of the words in verse 2 are monosyllables. But what profound truth: "Grace unto you, and peace." It would be difficult to find two words more meaningful than "grace" and "peace." These words represent God's answer to the greatest need of the human heart. Grace, a relationship between God and man, is established and based upon the fact that Christ died for sinners, resulting in God's unmerited favor — God giving to man the opposite of what he deserves. Grace gives eternal life and blessing and promises for joy throughout eternity instead of judgment which man justly should have. Coupled with grace is peace. How the human heart longs for peace. There is, of course, so much involved in this word. All Christians have peace *with* God. The enmity or the wrath of God has been put aside for us and we are the objects of His favor. There is also the possibility for Christians to have the peace *of* God, the *experience* of peace. It is probable that this is what is meant in this passage of Scripture. He wanted them not only to have the realization that everything was right between them and the Lord, but that they might experience the peace of God in their trials and afflictions. Paul is reminding the Thessalonians that though they were in trouble and persecution they were, nevertheless, the recipients of God's wonderful grace and His satisfying peace.

THANKSGIVING FOR THEIR GROWING FAITH

In verse 3 Paul bears testimony to them, as in the first epistle, that they had been faithful to God in all their troubles. "We are bound to thank God always for you, brethren, as it is meet [fitting], because that your faith groweth exceedingly, and the charity [love] of every one of you all toward each other aboundeth." Because of the tidings of their faithfulness in trial, he writes, "We are bound to thank God." The word for "bound" is the word for paying a debt. He is saying that he owes it to them to thank God always for them. Certainly thanksgiving is fitting. Sometimes Christians forget to thank God for things He has done for them.

Two things in particular are occasions for thanksgiving — their faith and their love. He writes, "because your faith groweth exceedingly" (v. 3). The Thessalonian Christians had come to know Christ as Savior only a few months before. It was true from that moment on that they believed in God and in Christ. But Paul is not talking about the fact of their faith. The reason for his thanksgiving is that their faith had grown.

How is it possible for one's faith to grow? Is not faith in Christ as Savior enough? It is enough for salvation, but there is still room for deeper experience. While a Christian will not question the deity of Christ and the sufficiency of His wonderful salvation provided through His death and resurrection, it is possible to learn by experience really to trust the Lord concerning *all* things. That is a process of spiritual education. As Christians go through life, they learn to trust God. They find by experience that He is altogether trustworthy and that they can not only trust Him regarding eternity but can also trust Him about time. In other words, it is possible to grow in faith, and the area in which one trusts God increases.

It is a remarkable factor in personal experience that some Christians are perfectly willing to trust God about eternity, but the little problems of today and tomorrow seem too big to commit to the Lord. It is, of course, unreasonable and ridiculous to trust God about eternal things and not to trust Him about temporal things, but that is human nature. The Thessalonian Christians, however, were in a position where they had to trust God from day to day. They were in danger of their very lives. In this situation their faith grew, and that is what trial does for us. Tribulation works patience, patience experience, and experience hope (Rom. 5:3-4).

THANKSGIVING FOR ABOUNDING LOVE

Not only did their faith grow, but Paul writes, "the charity [love] of every one of you all toward each other aboundeth." It is one thing to trust the Lord; it is something else to have a true love for the brethren. Sometimes in our churches there is little evidence of heresy, but there is also little evidence of love for the brethren. The Scriptures bear witness that in the Thessalonian church the believers not only increased in faith, but they also had love one for another and love which abounded. In many ways this Thessalonian church was an ideal Christian assembly.

THEIR EXAMPLE BEFORE OTHER CHURCHES

In verse 4 Paul continues, "So that we ourselves glory in you in the churches of God." He uses the Thessalonian church as an illustration. "We glory in you in the churches of God for your patience and faith in all your persecutions and tribulations that ye endure." To faith and love he adds the virtue of patience. The word for "patience" is a very significant word in the Greek New Testament. The word used here is the word for "remaining under." Christians have burdens and cares and sometimes would like to get rid of them. It is possible to become impatient with a situation. The person who is patient "remains under" and he keeps carrying the load that is given him, and adjusts himself to the circumstances in which he is required to live. He regards his lot as something that God has given him. These Thessalonian

Christians are described as having a testimony that grows, a love that increased and abounded, and a patience that continued. This certainly is a marvelous testimony.

Having presented to them their resources and blessings in Christ, Paul contrasts their situation to that of their persecutors in verse 5: "Which is a manifest token of the righteous judgment of God, that ye may be counted worthy of the kingdom of God, for which ye also suffer." Here is a profound principle though it is not stated explicitly in this verse. For the Christian the present age is a day of suffering, a day of trial, a day of temptation, but in the future the glory will be ours. It is the pattern which Christ Himself went through, suffering first and the glory following.

The pattern for the world is just the opposite. The ideal for the world is eat, drink, and be merry now, for the suffering will follow. Judgment will come later. The Thessalonians were in trial now, but this was to them the evidence of their future glory. The very fact that they were in trial caused by their persecutors was the token or sign that their persecutors were going to be tried in the future.

The result for them was that they were going to be counted worthy of the kingdom of God for which they were suffering. The first part of verse 5 can be considered parenthetical: "the charity of every one of you all toward each other aboundeth . . . that ye may be counted worthy of the kingdom of God."

The Coming Judgment of God on the Wicked

In verses 6-9 the judgment upon the wicked is portrayed: "Seeing it is a righteous thing with God to recompense tribulation to them that trouble you; and to you who are troubled rest with us, when the Lord Jesus shall be revealed from heaven with his mighty angels [angels of might], in flaming fire taking vengeance on them that know not God, and that obey not the gospel of our Lord Jesus Christ: who shall be punished with everlasting destruction from the presence of the Lord, and from the glory of his power."

This portion of Scripture is very clear that the destiny of the wicked is something horrible to contemplate. The judgment of the living unsaved will take place at the time Christ comes back. The character of that judgment is plainly portrayed. It will occur when Christ returns to earth with His holy angels. It is a judgment of "flaming fire, taking vengeance on them that know not God . . . who shall be punished with everlasting destruction from the presence of the Lord, and from the glory of his power." It is true that the Thessalonian believers were going through trials, but the prospect before them was one of glory, one of reward, and one of blessing. The prospect before their persecutors was one of terrible judgment from God, as is pictured here in Scripture. Once again the contrast is drawn between trial and trouble as it comes to the Christian, and the just judgment of God which will overtake the wicked who do not obey and believe the gospel.

THE COMING OF THE LORD

The time for this judgment is revealed in verse 10: "When he shall come to be glorified in his saints, and to be admired [or wondered at] in all them that believe (because our testimony among you was believed) in that day." In the Scriptures in general and in Thessalonians particularly a contrast is drawn between the coming of Christ for His church, which is pictured in 1 Thessalonians 4, and the coming of Christ to set up His millennial kingdom. At His coming for His church, according to 1 Thessalonians 4:13-18, the dead in Christ will rise first and living Christians will be caught up to be with the Lord. It is revealed in John 14 that after the church is translated Christ will take her to heaven to be with the Father in the Father's house in the place which Christ has prepared. This is the glorious prospect for the Thessalonians as well as for us.

In the Thessalonian epistles the coming of the Lord to the earth to set up His kingdom is also revealed. This event is not the same as His coming for His church. The question arises in verse 10 as to which coming is being discussed. The best explanation seems to be that in this verse Christ is referring to the coming to establish His kingdom. When He comes to take His church home to glory, the earth is not judged. The church is taken out of the world very quickly — in a moment, in the twinkling of an eye — and is taken to heaven. Christ also goes back with the church to heaven. It is not His purpose to judge the wicked then.

When He comes back to establish His kingdom, however, the Scriptures make it quite clear that He will judge the world in perfect righteousness. This judgment is illustrated in Matthew 25, where He gathers the Gentiles before Him and separates the sheep from the goats, that is, separates the saved from the lost. This judgment has to do with the living people in the world at the time of His second coming. In Ezekiel 20 the fact is revealed that He will judge the Jews in a similar manner when He regathers them from all over the world and purges out the rebels from among them. In other words, when Christ comes back it will be a time of separation of the wheat from the tares. He will separate the saved from the lost.

The very fact that He is coming back in such power and glory will result in many marveling at the power and the glory of Christ. When He comes back He will be accompanied by the saints. The event will be such a tremendous spectacle that it will impel worship and admiration on the part of all who believe. This is described in verse 10: "When he shall come to be glorified in his saints, and to be admired [wondered at] in all them that believe." This will be true not only of the church, which is with Christ as His bride, but it will be true of all others who might be comprehended in the term *saints*.

THE NEED FOR PRAYER

In verse 11 an application of the truth is made to Paul's prayer life: "Wherefore also we pray always for you, that our God would count you worthy of this calling, and fulfill all the good pleasure of his goodness, and the work of faith with power." Future things are not made known to satisfy our curiosity, but with the purpose of presenting practical truth upon which we can base our lives. This is the point Paul makes here. He has reviewed their sufferings, and how God is able to take care of them. He has discussed how the wicked will be punished in due time. Then he makes a practical application. If this is our destiny, if there is glory ahead, if we are to be in the very presence of our glorious Savior, what an exhortation it constitutes to live for Christ right now! In verse 11 Paul is praying always for them that this may be fulfilled in their lives.

Paul must have had a very long prayer list and must have spent a great deal of time in prayer. The burden of his prayer was that God would count them worthy of this calling. He did not mean by this that they were worthy of salvation, because no one could be worthy of salvation. It is rather that, being believers in Christ with such a glorious destiny, they should have a life that was in keeping with this. They would in this sense be "worthy of this calling, and fulfill all the good pleasure of his goodness, and the work of faith with power" (v. 11).

GLORIFYING THE NAME OF THE LORD

The result to be achieved is given in verse 12: "That the name of our Lord Jesus Christ may be glorified in you, and ye in him, according to the grace of our God and the Lord Jesus Christ." In this portion of Scripture the ultimate goal of experience — whether it is testimony, or enduring tribulation as the Thessalonian Christians did — is that the name of the Lord Jesus Christ might be glorified in them. In other words, as they lived their lives, sometimes in real affliction and trial, they could nevertheless live them in such a way as to bring honor and glory to the Savior. As we face our lives, in different walks of life, in different opportunities for service, is it true of us, as it was of these Thessalonian believers so long ago, that our lives are the means of bringing glory to the Savior? Are we really manifesting Christ as His trophies of grace, that we belong to Him and that He belongs to us?

It is possible for a Christian to live in such a way as to bring glory to Christ. But what does it mean to bring glory to Christ? This is an expression often used but perhaps not always analyzed or understood as it should be. The Scriptures state: "The heavens declare the glory of God; and the firmament sheweth his handywork. Day unto day uttereth speech, and night unto night sheweth knowledge" (Ps. 19:1-2). What does it mean when it is said that the heavens declare the glory of God? The heavens declare that God is perfect. The heavens manifest His wisdom, His power, and His purpose in designing all creation for an intelligent end. The heavens are manifesting the glory of God in the sense that they reveal what God is and what He can do. But the heavens are not designed to reveal the love of God, the grace of God, nor the righteousness of God. That is where Christians come into the picture. We are designed to show ''the exceeding riches of his grace in his kindness toward us through Christ'' (Eph. 2:7).

If we are going to manifest the glory of God, we must become an illustration of what the power of God and the grace of God can do. Therefore, as we yield our lives to the Lord and seek to serve Him, we are able to glorify God. In other words, our daily life and testimony can be an example of what the grace of God can do for us. The result is that ''the name of our Lord Jesus Christ is glorified'' in us. An additional thought is given, however, that Christians are also glorified ''in Christ.'' This is more than simply the matter of our glorifying God. It is revealed not only that Christ can be glorified in us but that we can be glorified in Him. Just what does this mean? It is stated that we are in Christ, that we have this wonderful position which has been given to us because we have trusted in the Lord Jesus Christ. When Christ is glorified we are glorified in Him. This is His contribution to us and will be fulfilled particularly when He presents us in glory as the passage in closing indicates. However, it is all ''according to the grace of our God and the Lord Jesus Christ.''

THE CHALLENGE OF THIS CHAPTER

In this first chapter some of the practical things that undergirded the Thessalonian church have been considered. Paul's thanksgiving for their faith in the midst of persecution is declared. In contrast to their trouble, the coming judgment of the wicked is revealed. The chapter closes with their need for prayer. The Apostle Paul prays for them that in their trial and affliction they might truly manifest the glory of God in faithfulness and testimony.

What was true for the church at Thessalonica is certainly the standard for us today as well. God challenges our hearts as we face these Scriptures in this modern generation that regardless of our circumstances or difficulties we may live a life that is faithful, a life that is well pleasing in the sight of God, a life that brings honor and glory to His name.

Questions

1. What was the occasion of writing 2 Thessalonians?
2. Why does Paul include Silas and Timothy in his salutation?
3. What does Paul mean by grace and peace?
4. Why is Paul thankful for the Thessalonians?
5. What can be said of the example of the Thessalonian Christians?
6. What does Paul reveal about the coming judgment of God on the wicked and when will it occur?
7. What is the content of Paul's prayer for them?

CHAPTER 8

The Revelation of the
Man of Sin

SECOND THESSALONIANS 2:1-12

THE RISE OF FALSE TEACHING

The second chapter of 2 Thessalonians is one of the great prophetic chapters of the Scripture. No other chapter in the entire Bible covers precisely the same points of revelation that are given here.

The occasion for the new revelation was the rise of false teaching in the Thessalonian church. Because of their persecutions, some of the Thessalonians had begun to wonder whether they were not already in the Day of the Lord, the predicted time of divine judgment. If so, they realized that they were already in the time of tribulation, from which they had been promised deliverance in 1 Thessalonians 5. In answer to this false teaching, Paul not only gives them assurance that they are not in this period, but he also gives them definite signs, the character of which cannot occur while the church is still in the world.

In the opening verses of the chapter, this problem is considered: "Now we beseech you, brethren, by the coming of our Lord Jesus Christ, and by our gathering together unto him, that ye be not soon shaken in mind, or be troubled, neither by spirit, nor by word, nor by letter as from us, as that the day of Christ is at hand." Practically all scholars agree that a better translation of the closing phrase is, "that the day of the Lord is now present." In other words, they had been taught by someone that they were already in the Day of the Lord, that this fearful period of divine judgment had already overtaken them. This troubled them because it was not what Paul had taught them earlier.

THE ALLEGED REVELATION

The false teaching that had come to them by one of the three methods is mentioned in verse 2, by "spirit," "word," or "letter as from us." Some of them had claimed that the Spirit of God had revealed this to them as a special revelation. Paul flatly contradicts this as a teaching of God. He also denies that he had sent any word orally to this effect.

Further, he declares that he had not written it to them in a letter, "nor by letter as from us." Apparently, they had received a forged letter which claimed to be from the Apostle Paul, teaching that they were already in the Day of the Lord. He said in effect, "I did not write such a letter." The letter, if it was written, must have been a forgery. The teaching that they were then in the Day of the Lord is therefore labeled as false doctrine and their fears of being in this awful period are shown to be groundless.

What Is the Day of the Lord?

In order to understand the nature of the error Paul is correcting, it is necessary to define what is meant by the "day of the Lord." This expression is found often in the Bible. In a word, it is the period of time predicted in the Scripture when God will deal directly with human sin. It includes the tribulation time preceding the second advent of Christ as well as the whole millennial reign of Christ. It will culminate in the judgment of the great white throne. The Day of the Lord is therefore an extended period of time lasting over one thousand years. This is brought out in the events included in the Day of the Lord, presented in connection with the study of 1 Thessalonians 5.

Our present time is a day of grace. God is not attempting in our day to deal directly with human sin. He may impose judgment in some cases; but there are many wicked people who flourish, who have health and wealth; they may succeed in business, even though they are not Christians and are not honoring the Lord. The Lord is not attempting to straighten that out now. This is a day of grace. The purpose of God in this day is to proclaim His grace, that souls may be saved by trusting in Christ and receiving God's gift of grace.

In the Day of the Lord, however, God will deal directly with human sin. The Scripture clearly presents the fact that the Day of the Lord is a day of divine judgment upon the world. In the Day of the Lord Christ will rule with a rod of iron over the entire earth (Ps. 2:9; Rev. 2:27). He shall administer absolute justice (Isa. 11:1-9). In that day also Israel will be regathered (Isa. 11:10-12) and brought into the blessed peace of the millennial kingdom (Zeph. 3:14-20). In a word, there is a time of divine judgment coming, the Day of the Lord, in which God will deal directly with this wicked world.

Were the Thessalonians Already in the Day of the Lord?

The question which faced the Thessalonians, however, was whether their present sufferings were evidence that they were in this predicted period. Paul is answering this question in effect, "No, you are not going to enter that period. The Lord will come for you first."

In order to make this particular doctrine clear, some of the things that occur at the beginning of the Day of the Lord are revealed. Because these events had not taken place, it demonstrated that the Day of the Lord had not yet begun.

The Thessalonians could not be in the Day of the Lord because certain things had to happen first. Accordingly, Paul writes in verse 3: "Let no man deceive you by any means: for that day shall not come, except there come a falling away first, and that man of sin be revealed, the son of perdition."

The Predicted Departure From the Faith

Two things are mentioned in verse 3 as necessarily occurring before the Day of the Lord and the time of judgment can begin. The first thing that is mentioned is "the falling away," and the word translated literally is "the apostasy," which means a falling away or a departure in a doctrinal sense. Our English word *apostasy* comes from the very Greek word used here. Paul is writing them, then, that this Day of the Lord cannot come until there is a widespread departure from the true faith in God. Some have understood this "departure" to be the departure of the church itself — that is, the rapture. If so, it would definitely place the rapture before the tribulation. Most expositors have understood it as doctrinal departure, that is, apostasy.

At the time 2 Thessalonians was written there were, no doubt, some errors in the church, but there was no apostasy in the ordinary sense of the term. The churches were still true to the Lord. Paul is declaring that the Day of the Lord cannot come until there is a departure from the faith first. The Scriptures speak often of this coming apostasy. In 2 Timothy 3:13, it is revealed: "Evil men and seducers shall wax worse and worse, deceiving and being deceived.'" Again in 2 Timothy 4:3-4, it is declared: "The time will come when they will not endure sound doctrine; but after their own lusts shall they heap to themselves teachers, having itching ears; and they shall turn away their ears from the truth, and shall be turned unto fables." The Scriptures, then, predict that before this time of judgment can come, there must come first a turning away from true faith in God on the part of the professing church.

In the twentieth century the situation is entirely different than it was for the Thessalonian church. Today there is widespread apostasy. The sad fact is that there are many who are not preaching the true gospel and, moreover, are denying the central doctrines of our Christian faith. Some are teaching that Christ is only a man, that He did not rise from the dead, that salvation is not through His shed blood, and that He is not coming again. They deny that the Scriptures are the Word of God, and turn instead to some other forms of teaching. To a certain degree, apostasy is already here.

The Coming of the Man of Sin

The Scriptures indicate, however, that this present stage of turning away from the truth is just the beginning. It will culminate in that period called the Day of the Lord. The record declares that "that day shall not come except there come a falling away first, and that man of sin be revealed, the son of perdition." In other words, apostasy which today is general is going to become specific. It will be headed up in the particular person mentioned here as the "man of sin" or a man of lawlessness — a man who is opposed to God. He is called "man of sin" because this is his chief characteristic. Just as we refer to Christ as the "man of sorrows" because He was a man who had endured much sorrow, so this person is a man of sin. His very life is characterized by blasphemous sin against God.

The verses which follow describe the nature of that sin: "Who opposeth and exalteth himself above all that is called God, or that is worshipped; so that he as God sitteth in the temple of God, shewing himself that he is God." Many believe that this is a reference to the future world dictator, the beast out of the sea of Revelation 13. Others believe it is a reference to the false prophet (Rev. 13:10-18; 19:20), who is associated with him. In either case, the apostasy is embodied in a man who has not yet appeared. The Day of the Lord, therefore, could not have come because this evil person has not yet been revealed.

In verse 5 Paul adds this word: "Remember ye not, that when I was yet with you, I told you these things?" One of the remarkable facts about the Thessalonian church was that Paul had taught them so much in so short a time. When Paul came to Thessalonica, there was not a single Christian there. When he left Thessalonica after only three weeks of ministry, a small church had been formed. He had not only led them to Christ, but he had taught them some of the deep things of the prophetic word. Now he reminds them of it. Paul writes: "Remember ye not, that, when I was yet with you, I told you these things?"

THE RESTRAINER

In verse 6 another reason is given why they were not in the Day of the Lord: "And now ye know what withholdeth that he might be revealed in his time." The "he" refers back to this man of sin. The statement of verse 6 declares that there is something holding back the revelation of this man of sin. An obstacle is in the way which had to be removed before the Day of the Lord could begin.

In verses 7-8 the explanation is given: "For the mystery of iniquity doth already work: only he who now letteth will let [or as is translated in modern English, 'He who now restrains will restrain'], until he be taken out of the way. And then shall that Wicked be revealed, whom the Lord shall consume with the spirit of his mouth, and shall destroy with the brightness of his coming."

The "Wicked" one in verse 8 is another reference to the man of sin. He can be revealed only when that which restrains his manifestation is taken away.

What is being referred to in this passage as the one who restrains? In verse 6 the restrainer is described as an indefinite thing, "that which withholdeth" or "that which holds back." In verse 7 the restrainer is described as "he" — "only there is one that restraineth now, until he be taken out of the way" A.S.V.). The record seems to imply that this must be a person, but who is this person? Expositors have had a good deal of difficulty deciding just what is meant. Even the best of Bible scholars who honor the Word of God do not necessarily agree on the identity of the restrainer. Many explanations have been offered.

One interpretation is that the man of sin was Nero, the Roman emperor. He was so evil that he was restrained by Seneca until Nero contrived to have Seneca put out of the way. Then, of course, Nero was released and could do as he pleased. He burned many Christians at the stake and brought much persecution on the church. But evidently this explanation is not correct. The things which should follow the Day of the Lord, such as the second coming of Christ, have not occurred since. The man of sin could not have been Nero and the restrainer could not have been Seneca.

One honored scholar says the restrainer is Satan — that Satan is the one who is restraining evil. His idea is that Satan is holding back evil in its true character and that restraint will be removed in the time of the tribulation and then sin will be revealed in its true picture. There may be some truth in the fact that Satan does not always manifest sin in its real nature, as he is sometimes "transformed into an angel of light" (2 Cor. 11:14). Certainly the Bible does not teach that Satan actually restrains sin. The Bible from Genesis to Revelation teaches exactly the opposite. Satan is revealed as doing all the evil he can. Furthermore, Satan is not taken away during the tribulation when evil reaches its peak. This interpretation, likewise, is not correct.

Another very popular explanation is that the restrainer refers to the law and order which came out of the Roman government. The Roman government was evil in many ways, but it did preserve a certain amount of law and order. Adherents of this view visualized the removal of law and order in the tribulation period with the result that restraint of evil is taken away. They believe that the wicked one will be revealed then and sin will be brought out into the open. But this explanation is also inadequate. While the Day of the Lord is a very evil period, it will be a period of rigid government. There will be regimentation in that day such as we in America have never known. A government permit will be required to go to the grocery store and buy, and a government permit will be needed before one can sell. Government will not be removed in the tribulation. Human government will reach its peak of authority and power during this time. This explanation does not seem to fit the passage either.

THE RESTRAINER IS THE HOLY SPIRIT

Who is it, after all, that really restrains sin? The answer found in the Bible is that God is the one who restrains sin. In Genesis 6:3 it is declared that the Spirit of God was restraining sin in the days of Noah. It was predicted that instead of striving with sin God would judge it in the flood.

In the Book of Job it is recorded that Satan wanted to afflict Job, but God had built a hedge about him. Satan testified that he was restrained by God from trying Job. When Satan accused Job of serving God because God had been so good to him, God took down part of the hedge and permitted Satan to take away all of Job's property and all of his children in one day. He left Job only his wife and his own life. When the Lord called Satan's attention to Job's faithfulness in affliction, Satan said it was because God had preserved Job's health. Then God permitted Satan to afflict Job's body, but not to take his life. Satan then brought severe physical affliction upon Job, and Job was in torment in his body. But in it all Satan could not go any further than God permitted him. Satan was restrained by God Himself.

It would not be possible for any believer to do any work for God if it were not for God's protecting hand. It is God who restrains. God may use varying means. He may use the government which maintains a certain amount of law and order. In the end, it is God who does it. It is God who provides protection for the Christian.

More specifically, in this present age it is the Spirit of God who provides protection. As it is revealed in Genesis 6:3, the Spirit of God strives with men and opposes Satan and his program and his hatred of the children of God.

While the Holy Spirit has always worked in times past, on the Day of Pentecost the Spirit of God came in a special way. Christ, who had always existed and was always present in the world, came into the world, was born of the Virgin Mary, and in a special sense left the world when He ascended and went back to heaven, even though He said, "Lo, I am with you always." So also the Spirit of God came on the Day of Pentecost and now indwells the church and is present in the world. The Spirit will return to heaven at the rapture.

The most natural explanation of the taking away of the restrainer is to identify this particular action with the time when Christ will come to take out His church. If the Spirit of God indwells the church and the church is taken out of the world, then the Spirit of God will also be taken out of the world. This does not mean that the Spirit will not continue working in the world in some way; but it will mean a reversal of Pentecost. Just as the Spirit came on Pentecost, so He will leave when Christ takes the church out of the world.

The very removal of both the church and the Spirit from the world will release the world to sin as it never has before. The presence of believers in the world exerts a great influence upon the wicked world. Christians who have stood for civic righteousness and law and order will no longer be in evidence. For the time being at least, there will be no one except unsaved people to run government. The net result will be that evil will be manifested beyond anything known in the history of man. The "mystery of iniquity" is, of course, already working as mentioned in verse 7, but the Holy Spirit is now restraining sin until He is taken away at the translation of the church. When this occurs, it is revealed in verse 8 that "then shall that Wicked one be revealed, whom the Lord shall consume with the spirit of his mouth, and shall destroy with the brightness of his coming."

There are, then, three good reasons why the Day of the Lord and the tribulation time could not have begun in the time the Thessalonians lived: first, the apostasy had not come; second, the man of sin had not been revealed; and, third, the Spirit of God had not been taken away. In a large sense, those unfulfilled conditions are still true today. While there is apostasy in our midst, the man of sin has not been revealed, and the Holy Spirit has not been removed. All of this constitutes real evidence that the tribulation time has not come and that it cannot come until Christ comes and takes His church home to glory.

The Character of the Man of Sin

In verse 9, there is continued revelation of the man of sin. He is described as one "whose coming is after the working of Satan with all power and signs and lying wonders." The principle that is expounded in Scripture is that Satan works by limitation. He wants to be like God. As God has described in His Word that Christ and Christ alone can rule the world in peace and righteousness, and has proved the deity of Christ by the many miracles which He performed, so this man of sin will be Satan's man even as Christ is God's man. He will be promoted in the world and assume the role of a superman. He will be set forth as the outstanding leader who can bring the world out of its difficulties. His power will come from Satan himself and Satan will enable him to perform certain signs and lying wonders. They will not be on the same plane as the miracles which Christ performed, but he will be able to do what will seem to be supernatural. The world will say of him, "Who is like unto the beast?" (Rev. 13:4).

In the verses which follow, the working of Satan is described as accompanied "with all deceivableness of unrighteousness in them that perish; because they received not the love of the truth, that they might be saved. And for this cause God shall send them strong delusion, that they should believe a lie: that they all might be damned who believed not the truth, but had pleasure in unrighteousness'' (vv. 10-12).

UNBELIEVERS WILL BE DECEIVED BY MAN OF SIN

The Scriptures teach clearly that many will be deceived and will not receive Jesus Christ as their Savior. The man of sin will come as a substitute in place of Christ and people who resisted Christ and did not receive Christ will flock in great numbers to follow this evil character. This will come to pass, of course, in the time of the great tribulation. All of this is declared to be a judgment from God. Men will be deceived and perish ''because they received not the love of the truth, that they might be saved.'' ''God shall send them strong delusion.'' But how can God deceive a person? The answer is given in the context.

First of all, it is clear that those who are deceived had opportunity to receive Christ, but they did not do it. There seems to be a principle of divine justice here that when a person turns away from the truth God allows that one to be led off into error. So often when people depart from the truth it is because they have resisted the Spirit of God as He sought to lead them into the knowledge of the Word of God. So it will be in that day. Those who have turned away from Christ will turn instead to this false leader and thus believe a lie instead of believing the truth.

Some understand from verse 11 that if a person in this present age of grace hears the gospel and does not receive Christ as Savior, then when Christ comes and takes His church home to glory these will find it impossible to be saved after the church is translated. It is unlikely that a person who rejects Christ in this day of grace will turn to Him in that awful period of tribulation. But the usual principle of Scripture is that while there is life there is hope. It is possible, though very improbable, that a person who has heard the gospel in this present age of grace will come to Christ after the rapture. The Scriptures definitely teach that God will send strong delusion to those who do not believe after the church is gone. God will judge their hearts, and if they deliberately turn away from the truth He will permit them to believe a lie. They will honor the man of sin as their god and as their king, instead of acknowledging the Lord Jesus Christ. The result will be ''That they all might be damned who believed not the truth, but had pleasure in unrighteousness'' (v. 12).

THE DESTINY OF UNBELIEVERS

The awful destiny of those who turn away from the Lord Jesus Christ is presented in verse 12 so clearly. It is a sad fact that many today will not receive Christ. They are indifferent and turn away without trusting Him. It is so common that Christians often fail to realize how desperate the condition is of one who hears the gospel and turns away. The choice is not an unimportant alternative. Men are actually determining their eternal destiny. The person who turns from Christ finds himself in a path of total hopelessness. He is headed, as the Scriptures make very clear, into eternal punishment.

THE URGENCY OF PREACHING THE GOSPEL

This solemn truth should give to us all a sense of the urgency of our day to tell people about Christ. The great majority of people who are within the sound of the gospel today will not heed and turn to Christ. It is very evident that these will flock after this false leader and, instead of believing in Christ in that awful time of the tribulation, they will believe a lie and go on to their eternal damnation. But in this day of grace Christians have a real commission. The climactic days of the Day of the Lord will not come until Christ comes for us first. While we wait we certainly should be challenged by the Lord to give our hearts and lives to Him. As God enables us to proclaim the gospel, the message should be sent forth that Christ loves those who are lost and died for them, that He is able to save if they will come to Him. Christians need not fear the coming of this tribulation time, for we have the hope of His imminent return.

Believers may have trouble in this world and some have gone through awful testings. There have been tens of thousands of martyrs in our generation. But this is not the Day of the Lord; this is not the time of tribulation. This is still the day of grace. God is still waiting for lost men to come to Him. One of these days the last soul will be added to the church, and the church — the body of Christ — will be complete. When that last one accepts the Lord Jesus, at that very moment the Lord will come for His church, and the completed body of Christ will be caught up to be with the Lord. Then will follow, as the Scriptures make so very plain, this awful period described as the Day of the Lord — the time when God's judgments will be poured out upon an unbelieving world.

The obvious lesson from this portion of Scripture is that we should examine our own hearts. Have we really trusted Christ? Have we been born again through faith in Him? If we have not trusted in Him before, now is the time to put our faith in Him. If we take this step, we can look forward with every other Christian to the coming of the Lord. That is our hope. We need not fear the coming of the Day of the Lord for when that day comes on earth we will be with the Lord in glory.

Questions

1. What was the nature of the false teaching which had troubled the Thessalonians?
2. How does this relate to evidence that Paul had taught they would be raptured before the Day of the Lord?
3. What is the first future event which Paul says must occur before the Day of the Lord is clearly come?
4. What is meant by the expression "the falling away"?
5. To what extent will there be apostasy before the day of the Lord and how is this in contrast to apostasy after the Day of the Lord begins?
6. How is the man of sin described and how does he relate to end-time apostate leaders?
7. What is the second major event which must take place before the Day of the Lord comes?
8. What is the significance of the expression "the restrainer"?
9. In what sense is "the restrainer" taken away?
10. How does the taking away of the restrainer relate to the rapture of the church?
11. How does this teach that the rapture takes place before the Day of the Lord begins?
12. Summarize the three reasons why the day of the Lord and the tribulation still remain unfulfilled.
13. What further description is given of the man of sin in verses 9-12?
14. What is indicated about unbelievers who are deceived by the man of sin?
15. Why is it so urgent to believe the gospel today and what are the dangers of unbelief?

CHAPTER 9

Chosen to Salvation
SECOND THESSALONIANS 2:13-17

CHOSEN FROM THE BEGINNING

Having laid before the Thessalonians the wonderful hope of the coming of the Lord, Paul now takes up the immediate task of living for God. While waiting for Christ to come for His church, there is a task to perform, a life to live, a testimony to give. These things should be our present concern.

In verse 13, thanks is given to the Lord for having chosen these Thessalonian Christians: "But we are bound to give thanks to God always for you, brethren beloved of the Lord, for that God chose you from the beginning unto salvation in sanctification of the Spirit and belief of the truth." The revelation that is stated here so simply is one of the most profound doctrines of the whole Word of God. In fact, it is more difficult than the subject of the coming of the Lord. Our salvation did not originate in human choice. God willed our salvation long before we ever came into existence. This divine choice was based upon divine love and divine determination. Paul gives thanks because they were "brethren beloved of the Lord."

One of the great truths of Scripture is that before we ever had sense enough to love the Lord the Lord loved us. This is stated in the very familiar text, "For God so loved the world." Some would like to make these words read "God so loved the elect." God does love the elect, but that is not what the text says. God loved the world. He loved the unsaved. He loved them all. That is why He gave His Son. The love of God is mentioned often in Scripture. In 1 John 4:10, it is written: "Herein is love, not that we loved God, but that he loved us, and sent his Son to be the propitiation for our sins."

Likewise, out of His heart of love there was a divine decision in eternity past which is referred to here as our being chosen. The original act in our salvation was with God, not with man. When God chose us to salvation, He did not choose us because we were lovely. He did not choose us because He saw something in us that He did not see in others. But He chose us because He loved us.

There is a mystery connected with this revelation that none can ever completely fathom. Why did God choose us? We never will completely understand it, but the glorious fact is that He did. In Ephesians 1:4, this choice is described: "According as he hath chosen us in him before the foundation of the world, that we should be holy and without blame before him in love." The precious truth is that God chose us. This is the occasion of the thanksgiving in verse 13.

The testimony of the Thessalonians showed clearly that they were the chosen ones of God. In 1 Thessalonians 1:4 Paul had written earlier, "Knowing, brethren beloved, your election of God." So here again the believers at Thessalonica are reminded of God's grace in their election and salvation.

SANCTIFICATION OF THE SPIRIT

The process by which God chose these Christians at Thessalonica from the beginning, and how they are brought unto salvation is revealed in the next phrase, "Through sanctification of the Spirit and belief of the truth." What does "sanctification of the Spirit" mean? The simplest definition of true sanctification is that it means *to set apart as holy to God*. How has God sanctified those who once were bound for eternal punishment, once were without God, without hope, and under the wrath of God? How is it possible to take such a one and make that one sanctified by the Spirit?

Christ spoke of this tremendous process in John 16. He was dealing with His disciples on the necessity for His going away. The disciples did not want Him to go away and He then told them: "Nevertheless, I tell you the truth; It is expedient for you that I go away: for if I go not away, the Comforter will not come unto you; but if I depart, I will send him unto you. And when he is come, he will reprove the world of sin, and of righteousness, and of judgment: of sin, because they believe not on me; of righteousness, because I go to my Father, and ye see me no more; of judgment, because the prince of this world is judged" (John 16:7-11). These verses, so significant in their revelation, teach that when a person is coming to Christ there must be a work of the Spirit in his heart before he can come. That is the convicting work of the Holy Spirit. The Holy Spirit enables a person lost in sin to understand the truth of the gospel. The ministry of the Spirit is not to convict of sins (plural). The purpose of the ministry of the Spirit is not to make us realize what awful sinners we are. That may be a part of the process, but that is not the point. What the Spirit desires to impress upon an unsaved person is the one fact that he is not saved because he has not believed. It is the sin of unbelief, defined in verse 9, "of sin, because they believe not on me." The Holy Spirit must bring a person to the place where it is realized that the one obstacle standing between a lost soul and eternal salvation is lack of faith in Christ. One is not lost because one has not trusted Christ. It all comes to the focal point of simply trusting in the Savior.

The passage explains further the ministry of the Spirit: "Of righteousness, because I go to my Father and ye see me no more" (John 16:10). While Christ was on earth He was the living embodiment of righteousness. As people studied His life and saw what He did, they beheld the righteousness of God in action. But Christ is not here to tell us about righteousness. Unsaved people must be instructed on the subject of unrighteousness by the Spirit of God. They must learn, of course, that God is righteous. But they need to know most of all that God is able to give righteousness, to justify those who are willing to trust in Christ. God bestows a justification, a righteousness which is by faith — the free gift of God, purchased for us by Christ on the cross. A person who trusts in Christ can receive this righteousness. It is the ministry of the Spirit to make this truth plain.

The passage in John 16 speaks also of the fact that "the prince of this world is judged." This is a description of the victory over Satan at the cross. Christ won the victory over Satan by His death, and Satan is judged now. Satan is defeated by the death of Christ and his doom is assured. Back of sanctification is the work of the Spirit in bringing a person to the place where he sees that he is saved by simply trusting in Jesus Christ.

When a person trusts in Christ, then the work of sanctification really begins. First, there is the work of regeneration. In John 3, where Christ talked to Nicodemus, He said, "Ye must be born again" (John 3:7). "Except a man be born of water and of the Spirit, he cannot enter into the kingdom of God" (John 3:5). The person who once was lost and spiritually dead now becomes alive and receives a new nature in Christ. As such he is made fit to be set apart as holy to God.

Another phase of the sanctifying work of the Spirit is His ministry as He comes to indwell us. In 1 Corinthians 6 Paul reminds the worldly Corinthians that if they are really saved their bodies are the temples of God: "Know ye not that your body is the temple of the Holy Ghost which is in you, which ye have of God, and ye are not your own?" (1 Cor. 6:19). In other words, Paul is saying that every Christian is a sanctuary of God, that God has seen fit to take up His dwelling place in that person. This is a marvelous truth and a part of the sanctifying work of the Holy Spirit. Because of the presence of the Holy Spirit in Christians, they are sealed by the Spirit. His very presence is God's seal, God's token of ownership, God's token of security in Christ. In Ephesians 4:30, the exhortation is given: "Grieve not the holy Spirit of God, whereby ye are sealed unto the day of redemption." The day of redemption is the day of resurrection of believers. It is the day when the bodies of believers will be redeemed. As far as our souls are concerned, we are redeemed right now, but our bodies are not yet redeemed. According to the

Scriptures, the presence of the Spirit is God's token to us, the promise that we will be saved completely and transformed on that day of the redemption of our bodies.

In 1 Corinthians 12:13, still another aspect of the sanctifying work of the Spirit is revealed. There it is stated: "By one Spirit are we all baptized into one body, whether we be Jews or Gentiles, whether we be bond or free; and have been all made to drink into one Spirit." The very moment one is saved, the Spirit takes that person out of his position in Adam — in sin and under condemnation — and puts him in Christ, i.e., in the body of Christ, so that he is a living part of the organism we call the true church. That again is part of the sanctifying work of the Spirit. In addition to all that God provides for the individual in Christ in salvation, is the possibility of being filled by the Spirit as we yield ourselves to Him. The Holy Spirit works in us the divine character that God has ordained, and the fruit of the Spirit — the love, and the joy, and the peace — become our portion. Paul's thanksgiving for the Thessalonian Christians is because God has chosen them to salvation through sanctification of the Spirit.

Belief of the Truth

The last part of verse 13 brings out another great truth: "Through sanctification of the Spirit and belief of the truth." This verse has a very significant order. It begins with God and the process is carried through by the Holy Spirit. What was the part of the believer? It is stated simply, through "belief of the truth." On man's part, salvation and sanctification come because he is willing to trust in the Savior. This is a wonderful truth. It delivers the soul from legalism. It makes clear that it is impossible to build a ladder to heaven by some sort of good works, religion, or church ordinances. There is a proper place for works, but they are not the way of salvation. Works pertain to the Christian life and testimony, but salvation is something which God has to do for us.

It is to this glorious salvation that Paul tells us we are called: "Whereunto he called you by our gospel to the obtaining of the glory of our Lord Jesus Christ" (v. 14). They were called by the gospel, the means that God used to bring about the fulfillment of His choice, by the sanctifying work of the Spirit, and by their belief in the truth. We are reminded again how the Apostle Paul is jealous for the gospel. In Galatians he pronounces a curse upon anyone who does not preach the true gospel. He believed in putting the gospel first. In 1 Corinthians 15:1-4 he tells the Corinthians that when he came to them he declared unto them first of all the gospel which he defines: "how that Christ died for our sins according to the scriptures; and that he was buried, and that he rose again the third day according to the scriptures."

One of the tragedies of Christianity in our modern day is that there is so little clear preaching of the gospel. What is the good news? What was the message that led these Thessalonian people to know Jesus Christ as Savior? The good news was that Christ the Son of God had come and that He had died on the cross for the sins of the whole world. The good news was that though He was buried, He was raised the third day from the grave in newness of life, in victory over the grave, in evidence that He was indeed the very Son of God. It was a demonstration of the power of God and of the deity of Christ's own person. It was evidence of the fact that when He died He really had accomplished that which only an infinite person could accomplish — our eternal and infinite redemption. This is the true gospel.

The Coming Glory

As Paul writes this letter, he thinks back to the time when he had told the believers at Thessalonica these truths, and how they believed them. Through believing the gospel, they had become gloriously and wonderfully saved. But Paul also takes a look at the future, "to the obtaining of the glory of our Lord Jesus Christ" (v. 14). The Thessalonian Christians were in great affliction. They were going through real persecution. As Paul lifts up their eyes beyond their circumstances, he is reminding them that they are bound for the glory of the Lord Jesus Christ. The Scriptures declare plainly that before God gets through with us everyone of us will be perfectly glorious. We are going to be trophies of the grace of God. Through eternity, the church will be singled out as the example of what the grace of God can do, by taking poor, hell-bound sinners and transforming them into holy saints of God, conformed to the image of Christ. That is the glory. There are many imperfections evident in believers now, but when God completes His work the church will be a perfect bride for the Lord Jesus. There is glory ahead.

Exhortation to Stand Fast

On the basis of these wonderful truths and tokens of what God has done, in verses 15-17 an exhortation is given which is summed up in the words "stand fast." There is a natural tendency in the Christian heart to backslide. Against this we must stand. "Therefore, brethren, stand fast and hold the traditions which ye have been taught, whether by word, or our epistle" (v. 15). The word for "traditions" means *that which is given alongside*. Many commentaries have been written on the Scriptures. Men of God study the Bible and expound what it teaches. The commentaries are not inspired, and they are not infallible. Some expositors are very faithful in their exposition of the Scriptures, however, and it is certain that Paul was faithful as he expounded the truth of God. The teaching that accompanies the written Word, that which was given "alongside," should be held fast by Christians even though in others than the apostles their teachings are not infallible.

How we can thank God for faithful teachers and preachers of the Word! How much their teaching has contributed to the church! Paul says in reference to such teaching, "Hang on to it." The tendency in our day is always to be looking for something new and different. There is need to realize that truth is not new. H. A. Ironside used to say, "What is new is not true, and what is true is not new." In other words, it is the old truth that is true. We may find truths that as far as we are concerned are new. One can read the Bible and discover a new thought, only to find that others long ago had already seen the same truth. It was new truth to the individual even though it was old truth. Of course, we should endeavor to learn more of the Scriptures, but we should also hold fast the traditions, the things we have been taught.

Prayer for Their Comfort and Establishment

In verses 16-17 Paul closes the section with a prayer: "Now our Lord Jesus Christ himself, and God, even our Father, which hath loved us, and hath given us everlasting consolation and good hope through grace, comfort your hearts and stablish you in every good word and work." This portion of Scripture serves as a reminder of the place of prayer and how Christians need to let God have His way in their prayer life. The prayer is addressed to the Father and to the Lord Jesus Christ. It mentions how they have loved us and how they have given us "everlasting consolation and good hope through grace." On the basis of the prospect before them, they are to comfort their hearts and to be established in "every good word and work." In other words, their Christian life and testimony consists of what they say and do. Paul prays that they will be established, that is, be firm and faithful in the task that God has given. As we in our day face the challenge of our own lives, may these truths be not only for the Thessalonian church but may they grip our hearts. May we thank God that He did choose us. May we thank Him for the sanctifying work of the Holy Spirit. May we thank Him that someone gave us the gospel and that into our hearts there came faith in the Word of God and in the gospel of our Lord Jesus Christ. Let us thank God for all He has done to us, and that now our destiny is to have the glory of our Lord and Savior Jesus Christ.

Questions

1. What occasions Paul's renewed note of thanksgiving?
2. What further teaching does Paul give on sanctification?
3. How is sanctification related to John 16?
4. Summarize the important works of God that relate to sanctification.

5. How does Paul contrast their coming glory and their present persecution?
6. How does the fact of their coming glory give Paul a basis for exhorting them to stand fast?
7. What is the content of Paul's closing prayer in Chapter 2?

CHAPTER 10

Serving and Waiting

SECOND THESSALONIANS 3:1-18

In the closing portion of 2 Thessalonians 2, a tremendous revelation of the riches of our wonderful salvation was given — that God chose us in eternity past and saved us through the hearing of the gospel message as it was preached. Because of this, we have glory ahead. On the basis of these truths, Paul exhorted the believers at Thessalonica to stand fast and to continue in their Christian life and testimony.

EXHORTATION TO PRAY

The third chapter of the epistle presents some of the privileges and responsibilities which belong to a true believer in this age. This first exhortation is a reminder that all of us need: "Finally, brethren, pray for us, that the word of the Lord may have free course, and be glorified, even as it is with you: and that we may be delivered from unreasonable and wicked men: for all men have not faith" (vv. 1-2). The Thessalonians were in trouble and tribulation. Some of them probably were in danger of their lives because of their testimony for Jesus Christ. It was in this affliction and trial that Paul was trying to help them and comfort them by reminding them of the great verities of the faith. At the same time, he speaks of their continued obligation to serve the Lord.

While Paul was writing to them about their troubles and the Lord's comfort and help for them, he had been reticent about his own troubles. Paul, too, was having his difficulties. The task committed to Paul was a very lonely one: to go from place to place, frequently coming into a strange city where not one person would welcome him. He was not entertained in the best hotel, nor was there any honorarium for him in recognition of his services. He had to find his own way, arrange for his public meetings, and somehow try to bear a testimony for Christ. Apart from fellowship with the Lord, it was a very difficult and solitary task and one in which there were many discouragements.

With this as a background, without complaining or saying very much about it, Paul asks the church at Thessalonica to pray for him. In effect, he was saying, "Don't forget that I need your prayers, too. You are not the only ones who are in trouble. You are not the only people who need prayer." This was sound advice to the Thessalonians. One of the best ways for you to be helped to bear your own burden is for you to get under someone else's burden. If you realize that others have needs too, as you pray for them it will make your own load lighter.

Paul also really needed their prayers. He told them to "pray for us that the word of the Lord may have free course, and be glorified, even as it is with you." The average layman does not realize how much a preacher of the gospel is dependent upon the prayers of God's people. Whenever an evangelist or a Bible teacher attempts to expound the Word of God, he is not only contending against failure on the part of those who listen, but against the unseen powers of darkness. He is engaging in a spiritual warfare. All the powers of hell are arrayed against him. There is a battle on, spiritually, whenever one tries to do something for his Lord.

No one can win the battle alone. There never has been a preacher used of God who was not supported by God's people in prayer. Even an ordinary person without extraordinary gifts can accomplish a great deal if God's people pray for him. Paul was a great leader, and God had given him wonderful spiritual gifts, had marvelously called him to serve Him, and had used him. But Paul was first to confess, "I cannot do it alone. I need your prayers." So he writes them: "Finally, brethren, pray for us, that the word of the Lord may have free course, and be glorified, even as it is with you." Behind every victory for the Word of God there must be a victory in prayer. When calling on a certain college president years ago, I asked how things were going. His reply was, "We are going forward on our knees." That was the right answer. In the Lord's work, progress made when we are not on our knees does not amount to much. It must be progress in prayer.

In all our labor for the Lord, it is very important that we pray. God has not called everyone to be a great preacher, teacher, or leader. There are some who could not even teach a Sunday school class and do a good job of it. They just do not have the gifts. On the other hand, it is surprising what God can do with a person if he is willing. Some have more gifts than they realize and are just too timid to use them. But there is one thing which every Christian can do, and that is to pray.

Prayer is not a gift. It is the universal privilege of every child of God. God has given us the ability of speech, and He has also given us the privilege to talk to Him on our knees. The marvelous thing about prayer is that every Christian is on the same level. Some believers may know more than others, but in the work of praying each believer comes to God in the name of Christ. What more could anyone desire than that? The small child as well as the mature saint has equal access to the throne of grace. In writing the Thessalonians who were young Christians, perhaps too much occupied with their own needs, Paul urges them to pray.

PRAYER FOR DELIVERANCE

Prayer is effective in overcoming opposition. In verse 2, Paul writes: "That we may be delivered from unreasonable and wicked men: for all men have not faith." Sometimes in the Lord's work, we have the experience of opposition in our testimony for Him. It may be a very serious matter. If one were in any of the countries which Russia controls today, one would know what it is to have the opposition of unreasonable men. One would realize something of how Satan can use human beings to hinder the preaching of the gospel. This kind of opposition to the preaching of the gospel is not limited to Russia, however. It can also be true right here in the United States in one form or another. Even here men sometimes risk their lives in taking a bold stand for the gospel. We need divine deliverance as we preach the Word, not only from satanic power but also from instruments which are under the control of Satan. Our weapon is prayer.

How often we have to come back to the statement in Ephesians 6, "we wrestle not against flesh and blood, but against principalities, against powers," the forces of Satan behind the scenes. That is the real battle, and that is why in Ephesians 6:18 we are exhorted to be "praying always with all prayer and supplication in the Spirit." The victory is possible only through prayer.

This prayer is, first of all, for the Word of God and its power, and then prayer for deliverance from ungodly men.

A word of assurance follows in verse 3: "But the Lord is faithful, who shall stablish you, and keep you from evil." Christians are often unfaithful. Often we are disappointed in their promises and commitments. But we can depend on the Lord. God is faithful. One of the things that we learn through the various experiences of life is that, though we may be unfaithful, God is never unfaithful. We can always depend on God to do what He has promised to do. Paul reminds the Thessalonians that God will hear and answer prayer. God is faithful not only to answer prayer but He will "stablish you, and keep you from evil." It is another way of saying Romans 8:28, "All things work together for good to them that love God." Paul is here reminding the Thessalonians that even in their trials and tribulations God will work it out for their good and to His glory.

Paul anticipates their faithfulness in prayer in verse 4: "We have confidence in the Lord touching you, that ye both do and will do the things which we command you." Can others depend on us to do the right things? When the call to duty or worship comes to us, are we in our place? As he writes the Thessalonian believers, Paul has confidence that they will be faithful.

THE LOVE OF GOD

Having laid upon them this exhortation for prayer in verse 5, he directs them to a different channel: "And the Lord direct your hearts into the love of God." That is just a little phrase, but how much it says. We are in a world that has so many bids for our affection. The issue comes up as to what is first, God or our loved ones. It is not always easy to make a decision. Then there is the enticement of money. We are told in the Scripture not to love money. One does not have to be rich to love money. One could be very poor and still love money. The temptation to love things and power to do what money can do is a temptation. Another lure is the love of the world, the love of the pleasures of the world, the comforts of the world, and the appearance of the world. It is dangerous for a Christian to have his heart set on something other than the Lord.

Recognizing this constant temptation facing us in this life, Paul tells the Thessalonians, in the midst of their trials and troubles, and service for the Lord, they are not to forget to love the Lord. This is one of the most important things in life. The Lord is more interested in our hearts than He is in what we do, or what we give, or what we say. He wants most of all our love. If He has our love, everything else will fall in line. This is why Paul exhorts them, "Direct your hearts into the love of God."

PATIENT WAITING FOR CHRIST

Then Paul adds the last part of verse 5 which goes along with loving the Lord: ". . . and into the patient waiting for Christ." Once again he sets before them the goal of the Christian expectation. He does not say, "Now patiently wait for the Day of the Lord." Neither does he say, "Now patiently wait until the time of trouble comes." That is not the point. He says, "Patiently wait for the Lord." That is our expectation, and that is our hope.

On the basis of these exhortations, he then gives them a list of things that should be done by the Christian who is waiting for the Lord. Frequently in this epistle it has been indicated that a true attitude of expectation regarding the coming of the Lord carries with it a practical daily life. In other words, God did not intend for us, after we have learned the precious truth that Christ is coming back, to sit with starry eyes and folded hands and look up to the heavens. That is not what He wants us to do. He wants us to face the challenge of each day recognizing that it might be the last day before Christ comes. We should make every day really count for the Lord. Christ should be first in the day. We should do the things that He wants us to do. This is a practical point of view.

Accordingly, Paul exhorts the saints at Thessalonica: "We command you, brethren, in the name of our Lord Jesus Christ, that ye withdraw yourselves from every brother that walketh disorderly, and not after the tradition he received of us. For yourselves know how ye ought to follow us: for we behaved not ourselves disorderly among you'' (vv. 6-7). This is an illustration of the fact that as a Christian our life should have order. There were those in the early church, just as there are in modern times, who had a tendency to go off into some sort of abnormal experience, and they were not orderly in their lives. They are told to withdraw themselves from such brethren. He said that which should characterize a Christian life is order and reverence. There should be a respectful attitude toward things of God. This was Paul's own standard: "For yourselves know how ye ought to follow us: for we behaved not ourselves disorderly among you'' (v. 7).

THE COMMAND TO WORK

Paul brings up another aspect of practical Christianity: "Neither did we eat any man's bread for nought; but wrought with labour and travail night and day, that we might not be chargeable to any of you: not because we have not power, but to make ourselves an ensample unto you to follow us. For even when we were with you, this we commanded you, that if any would not work, neither should he eat. For we hear that there are some which walk among you disorderly, working not at all, but are busybodies. Now them that are such we command and exhort by our Lord Jesus Christ, that with quietness they work, and eat their own bread" (vv. 8-12). It seems that there were some in this Thessalonian church who had this attitude. They said: "Now the Lord is coming, and there is no use getting a job, or trying to earn our bread. I will eat at your house as long as you have food, and if you run out we will go to someone else. There is no use working because the Lord is coming." Once in a while we find people who are just about as impractical as that in relation to the coming of the Lord.

Paul says: "That is not what I taught you. While I was among you, I earned my own living and worked in order to provide the necessities of my life. I would not be dependent on you. I paid my own way. I provided my own food. Now I have set you an example. You should be providing for your own things. You should not be living at the expense of others."

Here is a proper Christian standard. But some have adopted the philosophy that the world owes them a living. This is not found in the Bible. The attitude of the Bible is just the opposite. The attitude of the Bible is that the world owes the Christian nothing, but that we owe the world something. We have something to give to the world. This does not mean that Christians should be opposed to any true social program which helps others. But we are not to take the attitude that the world owes us a living. Paul lays down the principle in verse 10: "If any would not work, neither should he eat." That was a simple method of getting folks to work. If they did not eat, they had to do something.

The very fact that they were idle had led them into all sorts of difficulty. Idleness is fertile ground in which the devil can sow seeds. Paul tells them that he hears "that there are some which walk among you disorderly, working not at all, but are busybodies" (v. 11). Usually the type of person who does not mind his own business is trying to take care of someone else's business. That was true in the Thessalonian church. Paul's exhortation was: "Get busy. Earn an honest living. Pay your own way. Take care of yourself." You will not have time, then, to be interfering with other people's business and making a nuisance of yourself in the church of God.

In verse 12 he says to them: "Now them that are such we command and exhort by our Lord Jesus Christ, that with quietness they work, and eat their own bread." In other words, do not make a big noise about it, either. Just quietly do the right thing, provide your own livelihood and eat your own bread. Do not expect someone else to feed you.

COMMAND TO CONTINUE IN WELL-DOING

Paul also has a word of exhortation for those who have been doing the right thing: "But ye, brethren, be not weary in well doing" (v. 13). Sometimes we can be weary in well-doing in the sense that we are physically tired. There is nothing immoral about that. But he means we should not be weary in well-doing in the sense that we want to quit well-doing. The temptation when we see others who are not doing the right thing is to say, "What is the use? I am trying to do the right thing and no one else is. I think I will quit." Did you ever have an attitude like that? There apparently were some in the Thessalonian church who were having a little trouble along that line, so Paul said, "Be not weary in well doing." Keep on being faithful in the task God has given you.

Further, Paul gives advice concerning fellowship with those who are disobedient: "If any man obey not our word by this epistle, note that man, and have no company with him, that he may be ashamed" (v. 14). This may be a difficult verse for us to apply today. Some Christians have overworked it to the point where they think there is no one good enough for them. That is a sad attitude, too. But, on the other hand, the verse teaches us that we should not pick as our associates and friends those who despise and disobey the Word of God.

It is surprising how much depends on our friendships. Young people as well as those who are older should choose friends among Christian people who love the Lord. Such a choice will save a lot of temptation and keep many heartaches away. It is a good idea for young people to limit their social engagements to those who are Christians, to those who love the Lord. It may cut down the circle of friendships, but the friendships that remain will mean something and will be worthwhile. It may save one from the heartache of a marriage that is not in the will of the Lord.

In writing these Thessalonians about a different matter, Paul states this principle. Do not have fellowship with those who will not listen to the Word of God. Paul is claiming for his epistle that it is the Word of God and to be heeded as a command of God. Have your fellowship with those who are in obedience to the Word of God and who are living according to its standards.

Then Paul adds a word of caution to them in verse 15: "Yet count him not as an enemy, but admonish him as a brother." Do not walk around with a halo that is a little misplaced, saying, "I am holy; you are not holy." You will never help your brother that way. But when there is a real moral issue and your brother refuses to obey the teaching of the Word of God, then there must come a separation. You cannot follow him and follow the Word of God at the same time. These exhortations are practical, but they are all linked with the command to be patiently waiting for the Lord's return. If we are patiently waiting for His return, we will be doing these things which are pleasing in the sight of God.

PAUL'S PRAYER FOR THEM

In verses 16-18, the other side of the picture is presented. Paul had started this chapter by commanding the Thessalonian believers to pray for him, and now he prays for them. There is a comradeship and a fellowship in prayer. In these three verses, there are three things for which he prays. In verse 16, he prays for their peace: "Now the Lord of peace himself give you peace always by all means." Paul then voices the second petition, "The Lord be with you all." Then, he certifies that the letter is genuine: "The salutation of Paul with mine own hand, which is the token in every epistle: so I write" (v. 17). It makes all the difference in the world whether the letter is genuine, whether it is the Word of God. So he reminds them that it is a genuine letter, written by an apostle, by the inspiration of God.

The third petition in verse 18 is both a prayer and benediction. "The grace of our Lord Jesus Christ be with you all." Consider these three prayer requests: the Lord's peace, that passeth understanding; the Lord's presence, never failing; and finally the Lord's grace, His attitude of love and favor toward us. Certainly of all men we are the most blessed. In spite of all our experiences of trial and trouble, when the Lord is on our side we have more than anyone else. It is far better to be a Christian in trial and difficulty than not to be a Christian and have all the luxuries and comforts that the world can offer.

This epistle closes with the prayer that the grace of the Lord may be with you all. As we come to the conclusion of this study, may the prayer of the Apostle Paul, given so long ago to these Thessalonian Christians, be ours. May the Lord's peace be our portion. May the consciousness of His presence be a daily, moment-by-moment experience. May ''the grace of our Lord Jesus Christ be with you all.''

Questions

1. For what does Paul exhort the Thessalonians to pray and how does this indicate the nature of our spiritual warfare?
2. How does Paul relate the love of God and waiting for the coming of the Lord?
3. Itemize the things that Paul says Christians should be doing while waiting for the coming of the Lord.
4. What importance does Paul place upon Christians working?
5. How does Paul recognize the danger of being weary in well-doing?
6. With whom does Paul say we should not associate?
7. What are the three petitions with which Paul closes this epistle?
8. How would you summarize the practical exhortations of 2 Thessalonians?